The Art of Embroidered
BUTTERFLIES

SEARCH PRESS

TO NEIL,

with love as absolute as the

beauty of butterflies.

The Art of Embroidered
BUTTERFLIES

Jane E. Hall

First published in Great Britain 2012

Search Press Limited
Wellwood, North Farm Road,
Tunbridge Wells, Kent TN2 3DR

Text copyright © Jane E. Hall 2012

www.clothofnature.com

Photographs by Roddy Paine Photographic Studio
© Search Press Ltd 2012
Natural history photographs © Jane E. Hall
Photographs of the artist © Neil Hall-McLean

Design copyright © Search Press Ltd 2012

ISBN: 978-1-84448-530-7

Page 1

Painted Lady butterfly resting on thistles (detail from 'Thistledown Summer', page 117).

Page 3

Holly Blue butterfly on ivy (detail from 'Silent as Light', page 58).

Pages 4–5

Brimstone butterfly resting amidst periwinkle (detail from 'Periwinkle Wood', page 94).

Page 6

Speckled Wood butterflies (detail from 'Spirit of the Woodlands', page 78).

Acknowledgments

First, special thanks to Neil for his encouragement and support in all my artistic endeavours.

Thanks to my parents, also, for their abiding love and support, and a sincere thank you to Clive Farrell, mentor and butterfly friend, for sharing his butterfly knowledge, regaling me with butterfly stories and generously allowing me to roam as free as a butterfly about his gardens, sketching, photographing and waxing lyrical. I also extend my thanks to Clive for patiently reading through my manuscript and alerting me to any lepidopteral faux pas! I have been fortunate to meet many worthies in the field of lepidoptery (often quite literally!) to whom I owe a debt of gratitude, meeting with me, as they have, with enthusiasm and encouragement in my pursuit of butterflies. In particular, I would like to thank David Dunbar for schooling me in the ways of butterflies and sharing many happy and fruitful butterfly expeditions with Neil and me. For the sheer inspiration of his scientific study and successful re-introduction of the Large Blue, I would also like to thank Professor Jeremy Thomas.

Thank you to Isabelle and Gary Marsh for magical days at their home in Umbria chasing butterflies, and to Stella and Brian Smith for happy times in gentle pursuit of butterflies in sunny France.

I gratefully acknowledge the team at Search Press, especially Katie Sparkes, Juan Hayward and Roz Dace, who have worked with me closely in accomplishing this book. Thank you also to Roddy Paine and Gavin Sawyer for their patient, professional skill in photographing my work.

Many thanks to Rob Bull for his continued skill and patience in framing and presenting my work, and particular thanks also to Sadie Harrison, the owner of 'Sunrise'.

Finally, special thanks to Janice, my sister-in-law: an inspiration as true as the most beautiful of butterflies, and to Rupert, for the little book of gold.

Contents

Butterfly Studies

Foreword

Gone are the days of our Victorian ancestors who amassed vast collections of butterflies; mounted dead specimens which, one may argue, provided valuable scientific insight, but to me they seem like nothing more than sad, fading shells compared with the glorious living, flying, dancing creatures themselves. I think in part that these old-style collectors (aurelians, as they were called) longed to somehow possess the fragile and fascinating beauties they beheld. Today, this yearning is largely assuaged by photography, painting and, yes, embroidery. However, in respect of the art and embroidery of Jane E. Hall, any preconceived idea of this skill set will be challenged.

To me, encountering Jane's artwork was a revelation, as it will be to many who pick up this book. Her profound love of butterflies and phenomenal skill as an artist and embroiderer will surely inspire many, though perhaps few will come close to achieving such artistry as Jane, a world leader in this specialised area.

It is said that 'wonder is the beginning of philosophy' and Jane's art will surely inspire the reader to look more closely, wonder and think. If enough of us do this it will lead to further and better understanding of the butterfly world and, ultimately, on to vital conservation of habitat before even more species are lost forever and we are condemned to mourn the loss of some of the most beautiful creatures on earth.

I have entrusted Jane with live butterfly pupae, enabling her to observe how they hatch and dry their wings in readiness to take flight. She has wandered in my wild flower meadows, woodlands and tropical greenhouses, camera and sketchbook in hand, but mainly using those extraordinary gifted eyes. All this I can feel pulsing through the book.

On one level this book will be a joy to possess and browse through, allowing the imagination to roam. On another level it is a unique and meticulous guide to the application of the artistic techniques involved. Jane never dictates, she just explains how she achieves things artistically and gently encourages the reader to take his or her own path.

Clive Farrell
Vice President, Butterfly Conservation
April 2012

Peacock butterfly (detail from 'Dreaming', page 110).

Introduction

'Butterfly', a word which speaks volumes to me, evoking a narrative in my mind that begins in childhood: 'once upon a play time', one sunny day in the garden, watching fairy-like creatures dancing from one flower to the next and, in my imagination, from one world to the next as, with swiftness of flight, they seemingly disappeared.

My imagination still dances between worlds with the butterfly, both focusing my eye on the wonders of our natural world and leading me beyond the seen to the imaginatively perceived. There is great joy in seeing, in using that sense seated in the eye to understand, to learn. But it is perhaps a joy transcended by the sense that lies beyond the eye: 'imagination'.

There are a venerable number of enthusiasts and experts who have observed, and continue to observe, the natural world with great science behind their eyes, realising and affirming valuable data, to whom, as an artist devoted to nature, I feel deeply indebted. My studio bookshelves are lined with volumes exploring their discoveries. Books full of amazing facts and illustrations to which I constantly refer as I evolve my artistic studies and interpretations. In unison with this creativity a certain and satisfying cerebral knowledge of my subjects is also evolving, but I am no expert in the field of natural history. Mine is a field of tousled grasses; a meadow in which to play. A field of dreams, where ideas and imagination take flight along with the butterflies. I do not feel tasked to render my subjects with great accuracy. Though I do observe them acutely, I observe beauty before science and feel inspired to translate it artistically rather than challenged to attempt to emulate it. Many of my studies do closely resemble their natural counterparts but I humbly concede that through my merits as an artist I can only begin to approach such beauty and aspire to honour it. To emulate it would be to recreate a miracle; measured against such a goal I am, indeed, a child at play.

Butterflies are, to me, nature's signature, synonymous with their beauty and fragility yet possessed of eternal strength and tenacity.

Large Blue (detail from 'A Spell Amongst the Wild Thyme', page 66).

'Butterfly' – I repeat the word in my mind, determined to define what it means to me as an artist as I begin to explore its prevalence throughout my portfolio, in the pages of this book. To me, the very word is spell-binding, conjuring up halcyon days in my mind. It is a meditative word; a mantra reflecting beauty into the mental space that the everyday concerns of life conspire to narrow, creating expansive imagery of wild meadows, the spangled light of woodlands, blue sky, the dance of flight. For me, it embodies the very spirit of my creativity.

Of course, much of my work is closely observational. I am often blessed to find myself amongst the butterflies, 'studying them in the field'. Rendering their likeness in sketchbooks, capturing their beauty through the lens of my camera; gathering my thoughts and observations together in my studio and expressing them in the art work that I evolve. Yet my dedication to butterflies goes far beyond artistic rendition, 'art for art's sake'. The butterfly is my muse: many artists are possessed of one; the butterfly is surely mine.

I am as surely not alone in my love of butterflies. From earliest times the butterfly has been celebrated and venerated in art, poetry and the spiritual belief systems of different cultures across the world. Representations of butterflies can be found in Egyptian frescos at Thebes, dating back as far as 3500 years, where they are considered not only illustratively as part of the natural landscape but also figuratively, depicting Egyptian belief in the afterlife of the human soul. Butterfly imagery has likewise been found on ancient artefacts from China, Japan and America. Butterfly goddesses reigned over ancient cultures, significantly Minoan Crete and Toltec Mexico. Yet perhaps nowhere was it more integral to a spiritual belief system than in Ancient Greece where the butterfly represented the metaphysic of an entire civilisation. The Ancient Greek word 'phsyche' defined both soul and butterfly, so inherent was the conviction that the emergence of the adult butterfly from its chrysalis represented the personification of the human soul.

Such power imbued to one of the world's most delicate creatures – power transcending civilisations to this day when, for many, both religiously and secularly, it continues to represent freedom, hope and spirituality.

Butterflies are not the preserve of spiritual art and belief; since man first glanced their beauty they have inspired all manner of

Summer days; nostalgic recollections of playing in the garden, hiding in the long meadow grasses beyond the garden gate and exploring neighbouring woodlands.

Right: perhaps most inspiring of all, beyond the sheer beauty of these delicate creatures on the wing, is their metamorphosis from caterpillar into butterfly. Arguably all artists are given to flights of fantasy but 'in fact' this process is beyond fantastical, presenting such mystery and wonder, my muse becomes even more beguiling.

I watched in awe as this exquisite metallic blue tropical butterfly, Morpho peleides, emerged from its jewel-green chrysalis case.

creativity. With their infinite variety of pattern, spectacular array of colour and the gentle drama of their flight, they have captured the imagination of fine artists through the ages: Jan Van Kessel, Bruegel, Van Gogh and Picasso, to name but a few, to modern-day artists such as myself (I humbly add) to name but one! Their imagery abounds in the decorative arts and all manner of ephemera. They have inspired fashion, fairytale, folklore and great literature, being the muse of such worthies as Shakespeare and William Blake.

Great energy is borne of gentle things; there is perhaps nothing gentler than a butterfly's wings. Those wings carry me both spiritually and physically deeper into the natural world, my broader inspiration to be an artist. Their habitat is my earthly paradise; where they thrive, I thrive, though sadly this is where their strength is most threatened. Ideal butterfly habitat is becoming scarce, encroached upon by the needs of modern man. Ecologically, the balance necessary for their survival is delicately held. They need plants, specific to each species, to provide food for their voracious young-caterpillar stage, shelter for their pupae, and nectar for their life on the wing. These plants need not only the space to grow, itself encroached upon by modern agricultural practice

and development, but the right conditions to grow in, threatened by land management (or lack thereof) and global warming. For the Large Blue, chalky, rabbit-grazed grassland rich in thyme and thriving with a very specific red ant; for the Orange Tip, cuckoo flowers and hedge mustard; for the White Admiral, honeysuckle and bramble. Equally as challenging to tidy suburban minds, though far more commonplace, nettles are beloved of some of our most delightful butterflies, including the Peacock, the Small Tortoiseshell and the Red Admiral. Nettles indeed – considered nothing more than unsightly, stingy weeds by many and treated, justly in their eyes, with contempt and decimation! I for one have grown to love them, and I hope that as you explore our 'butterfly world' with me through the pages of this book you too may find a little space for nettles, if not in your heart then in a corner of your garden.

Perhaps it is befitting that these magical creatures demand such alchemy in nature, but it is none-the-less worrying to those of us that love them that this 'spell' in modern history, one of massive food and fuel production, urbanisation and global warming, falls like a curse upon them.

Butterflies in nature

The wealth of detail borne on a butterfly's wings is breathtaking. To see their intricate patterning through magnification, to understand that it is made up of miniature scales, each of differing iridescent colour (much of which is read by our eyes through the miracle of light diffraction), all but defies belief. For me, it defines the sense of 'wonder'.

Then there are their perfectly formed bodies to consider, covered with delicate hair, shimmering as if dusted with sunlight itself. Their beautiful, shiny, variously coloured compound eyes are equally as astounding to consider. They are understood to enable the butterfly to read the colours and designs borne on the wings of their fellow species, appropriating their mood for both love and territorial battle. They are also adept at identifying very particular sources of nectar amidst fields of flowering choices. Equally as stunning are their delicate antennae and balletic legs. Their antennae, perfectly poised, can detect scent more acutely than the nose of the finest perfumer, the scent of their own kind being most seductive of all to them, beckoning their attention from miles away. The European Giant Peacock Moth can detect the seductive pheromones of a prospective companion from a distance of up to seven miles (about eleven and a quarter kilometres)! Their balletic legs that anchor them so exquisitely, each with five segments, not only hold them fast through summer breeze and tempest, but by way of gentle tapping also enable them to identify plants specific to the nutritional needs of their young, on which they choose to lay their precious eggs.

Beyond the visually observed lies the insight of science. Scientific study of the butterfly has afforded man valuable knowledge of evolution and genetic inheritance. Studies have advanced research in the field of medicine, specifically cancer, anaemia and viral infection. Even with a limited grasp of the science, I cannot help but be awed by such understanding and feel even more inspired by my muse.

I believe that there is no inspiration, artistically or otherwise, without a sense of wonder; without wonder there is precious little light in the world.

The uncommonly beautiful Common Blue butterfly at rest, displaying its intricately patterned underwings.

Metamorphosis

If not by way of their beauty alone, one can surely discover a sense of wonder by exploring their metaphysical journey from precious egg to resplendent life on the wing.

Having chosen a plant from nature's wealth of thousands that is specific to the nutritional needs of her offspring, the butterfly lays her eggs, hiding them preciously beneath its leaves or beautifully disguised at its tender tips. Depending on her species she will lay just one, or a host of hundreds.

Having emerged from its egg casing (a miniature work of art in itself, in my eyes superseding man's most fantastical architectural designs) the minuscule larva begins its voracious life. In its familiar guise of 'hungry caterpillar' it devours proportionately vast quantities of foliage, resting for enforced periods of retreat to slough off its skin as it grows too tight to suit.

Finally, after much gorging and the shedding of many ill-fitting caterpillar suits (up to fifteen in the extreme, more commonly four, rather like our 'fashion seasons'!), the caterpillar is ready to undergo its most miraculous change. Abandoning its life of gluttony and languor, the caterpillar knows, in the most determined sense, that the time has come to undergo a transformation like no other, and time is of the essence. Indeed, time is finite; it has just hours to complete nature's schedule. Empowered by an innate understanding of what it must do it hastens to find a quiet, safe place where it will begin the process of transforming from caterpillar into chrysalis.

This 'pupation process' takes time and great effort. Initially, the caterpillar weaves a silken cloth pad which it adheres to a suitable surface, from which it then proceeds to hang itself upside down. After two days hung awkwardly in this position it sloughs off its skin for a final time, this time emerging to bear no resemblance to its former self. It must now fully secure its hold by extricating the tip of its body (the cremaster), which is covered in tiny spines designed to mesh with silk fibres. Once free it sinks itself into the silken cushion that it wove as a caterpillar. Such great effort, expended by a lifeform devoid of sight, infirm, with seemingly no means of motivating any course of action. Momentarily its life hangs by a thread; rarely, however, does the chrysalis fail in this transcendental trapeze. Exhausted by its endeavour it will now rest, motionless (excepting the occasional defensive twitch), not breathing, not eating, apparently lifeless. Yet within this miraculous casing, the most extraordinary, mind-boggling metamorphosis is taking place; from earth-bound caterpillar to the resplendent flighted creature we call 'butterfly'.

I have watched in awe as the long-awaited emergence of the butterfly begins. One or two days before the spectacular event the designs and colours of the wings become visible through the now transparent chrysalis casing. The flourish with which the ultimate emergence takes place is breathtaking. First the head, then the back and base of the wings break free. Carefully it then releases its legs, antennae and proboscis. Still clinging upside down it then pulls itself up quite suddenly to hang from its empty palace, the chrysalis case. Crumpled like a piece of dampened, coloured tissue paper, its body engorged with life, the miracle is realised in full as it pumps

Six-spot Burnet caterpillar, its minute silky hairs glistening in the sun.

Facing page, top: Blue Morpho chrysalises, modelled in air-drying modelling medium and silk, shown resting sideways.

Facing page, bottom: Brimstone butterfly at rest, preparing to hibernate over winter.

I believe that there is no inspiration, artistically or otherwise, without a sense of wonder. Without wonder there is precious little light in the world.

this life force into its wings. In minutes they are full size, resplendent and as soft as gossamer. They must dry and harden; the butterfly must be patient a little longer before taking to the sky. It will repeatedly furl and unfurl them until it is certain that they have the strength to fly, at which moment the extraordinary cycle of life begins again with its first flight in search of honeydew, nectar and love.

A love story played out amidst sunshine and flowers, how could one fail to be seduced by such a tale? Alas it is a tale which, akin to our beloved fairytales, is not without menace; a brooding sense of danger. The sun does not always shine; butterflies must endure harsh weather and, of even greater menace, climate change. They must avoid predation by the greatest of adversaries: sharp-beaked and clawed beasties and, perhaps most insidious of all, the carelessness and wanton destruction of their world by man. Then there are the gruesome ways and wiles of parasitic fellows; flies and wasps, fighting, some may argue perhaps over-sentimentally, without honour, for their existence too. Species weaken and, tragically, some fail. There isn't always a happy ending.

I have embarked upon a personal journey, intent on telling the butterfly's story through the art work that I evolve. Through these pages I hope to share the passage of that very journey with you; one in which I delight at every turn. I hope that by way of this I may encourage you to cherish butterflies too and embark upon your own voyage of discovery and delight.

Butterfly Conservation

The butterfly veritably symbolises nature in the hearts and minds of many. It is widely regarded as an 'indicator species' to all concerned with ecology and nature conservation. Indicators of climatic change, the adverse effects of modern agricultural practice and habitat loss, their study is invaluable to understanding how to redress the fearful imbalance between man's need (and avarice) to advance food production, road networks and building programmes and the needs of the natural world itself, a world which we are inherently part of, not separate from. There are many outstanding individuals dedicated to this important cause, far more qualified than I to discuss the pertinent issues; indeed it would be impertinent of me to do so. Instead, may I point you towards 'Butterfly Conservation', a society pioneering great work in this field. More fittingly, I will continue in my voice as an artist in possession of limited scientific knowledge, discussing the subject through the art work that I evolve and in such language as is afforded me. Through imagination and creative technique, I explore the necessity to conserve our natural world by reflecting upon its beauty and considering its spirit, a spirit which, in my estimation, is eloquence itself.

Materials

Silk

Silk is the greatest component of my work, borne of nature itself, a lustrous element of the silk moth's metamorphosis, spun by the caterpillar before pupation. The cocoons of the farmed silk moth, *Bombyx mori*, provide much of the silk that is manufactured; Shantung and Tussore silk are made from the cocoons of related wild species.

Fabric woven from spun silk is possessed of the gentle sheen and delicate weight of butterflies' wings. It carries dyes beautifully, not dulling their colour or impeding their natural flow unless, that is, I choose to limit it by priming the fabric.

The materials that I use are chosen for their affinity with my inspiration — nature — and are invariably borne of it. Natural, pre-dyed silk is my best loved material, it translates into the natural sheen and weight of a butterfly's wing beautifully. It also has a natural thirst for the dyes which I use, emulating both the subtle and the startling colours that the wings display.

I enjoy working with raw silk fibres processed into soft, lustrous silk tops. Teasing out the fibres from their long, silky skein and drifting them in criss-crossing layers over a flat surface, I then bond them into a papery cloth, delicately translucent and useful for many applications from butterflies' wings to sky. The process of working with fibres that resemble soft mist and billowing cloud is, in fact, a joy in itself, before and beyond the satisfaction of any useful application that the resulting papery cloth may have.

The gentle rhythm of a dainty needle carrying filaments of rainbow-coloured thread through sheeny silk is, to me, hypnotically soothing.

Silk threads

Silk threads, floss and plied, are a delight to work with. I favour the lightest weight, 20 and 40 denier plied threads, that are of limited availability today. When colour availability limits artistic expression, I ply my own threads from more widely available flat silk floss, still popularly used in Japanese embroidery. When this combined rainbow selection does not range to the 'butterfly scale' of colour I choose, I dye the thread myself.

Dyes

The dyes that I use are proprietary silk dyes, colour- and light-fast, though the resulting work is not machine washable at 40°C as the manufacturer suggests! I use them as a watercolourist uses paint, at times allowing colour to flow and merge, at other times pre-treating the fabric with a watercolour primer to prevent the colours from flowing, allowing me to control pattern and shape with the precision of a miniaturist.

Sets of dainty painted silk wings of the Speckled Wood butterfly rest alongside the fine silk thread with which I will detail their speckled brown scales.

Needles

The needles with which I work are very fine. Handmade by Japanese craftsmen, they have perfectly round eyes and sleek, flat heads. The gentle round eye is designed to carry the thread without bruising it, the flat head to carry the thread through fine fabric with equal gentility.

Magnifier

Working with such delicate elements and observing such minute detail, I often find it necessary to use magnification, most usefully a large, floor-standing magnifier with an attached halogen daylight bulb. I can angle and poise it over my work wherever I am seated, be it at my desk or comfortably resting in my great-grandmother's nursing chair, one of my favourite places in which to meditate and stitch.

Frame

The embroidery itself is supported on a large, floor-standing frame which is superbly adjustable for height and angle. It is imperative that one is sitting comfortably at work, which absorbs time as dry earth does rain. I estimate that the longest I have spent on any single resolved piece, a dainty butterfly amidst its setting, is upwards of a year.

Fine wire and paper clay

Fine wire affords my butterflies' wings their strength. Caught into the stitches on their undersides, it enables me to lift them into life. Observing the veining of a butterfly's wings in nature unlocks the secret to their strength. By the simple, more practical than magical, means of wiring, I artistically describe what I observe. Nature is my constant teacher.

The butterflies' bodies are crafted from paper clay or Model Magic®, air-drying modelling mediums which I work with fine tools. I observe their dainty natural form before brushing them with silk fibres resembling fine hair and painting them appropriately.

For their antennae I once again exploit the usefulness of fine wire, dipping its ends into a wet slip of paper clay to achieve their clubbed ends. With great precision I then push them into pre-formed holes in the modelled bodies. This is one of the many processes I exploit that can leave me quite breathless as I unconsciously hold my breath to still my mind and my hand. One must be patient and careful with tiny things and prepared to fail in their achievement every now and then. Human hands are clumsy indeed compared with the creator of such miracles as the butterfly. Nature constantly reminds me of how miraculous it is as I aspire to honour it through my creativity.

My studio

To inhabit a space which is conducive to creativity is a real joy and a great blessing. My studio rests within the bounds of our two-acre field, beyond which there is no visual boundary to the wide-open countryside beyond. I have aspired to such a space since childhood, when sheets and pillowcases tied to trees sufficed for ceiling, windows and doors. Pine needles and leaves made for exquisite carpeting (throughout of course!) and logs made up a charming three-piece suite. Variously, from play days to present day, I have perched at kitchen tables, 'camped' behind the sofa in makeshift studio style; I've even rested my workbox at the foot of my bed. Consequently, I feel even more tangibly blessed to have realised the dream of having a studio; a grown-up playhouse of my very own!

However, as a great man of literature once exclaimed: 'The very best place to work is in one's head'. A lack of space need not deter one from creativity. Liberate the time, find the mental space, and the absolute necessity for the ideal environment will fall away.

Standing proudly along the wall of my studio is my 'admirable double plan chest'. Of great provenance, it once belonged to renowned embroiderer, Constance Howard. I feel honoured to own it and have recommissioned it as the ultimate treasure chest! In it I store much that is useful, and much I simply consider beautiful. In one drawer I store my paper, my favourite of all being handmade. In another I keep watercolour paints, pencils, dyes and modelling materials. In yet another, threads, vintage fabrics, embroidered heirlooms, buttons and braids. There is one drawer for working drawings, swatches, sketches and photographs and one for work in progress. The remaining drawers, to me most delightfully of all, are dedicated to 'collections of things' that, if not directly, in a more abstract, aesthetic sense inspire my creativity.

In countless workboxes — old cheese boxes, matchboxes, shoe boxes, baskets, trays and drawers — I have treasured away every kind of useful thing pertinent to my work, at times somewhat stretching the definition of 'useful'. Through the pages of this book I will share many of these 'useful things' with you.

I often use magnification, most usefully a large, floor-standing magnifier with an attached halogen daylight bulb, both of which I can angle and poise over my work. The embroidery itself is supported on a large, floor-standing frame which is adjustable for height and angle.

These collections are arranged in old printers' trays and little boxes which, mosaic-like, fill the spaces in between, reaching far into the dusty corners of the drawers. They comprise all sorts of curious delights, many of which have been gathered (judiciously I may add) from nature. There are seashells, some gathered while beachcombing as a child, some from distant shores. There are smooth pebbles, rugged little rocks and 'lucky stones'. There are tumbled gems, vials of sand, lichen, moss and squirrel-nibbled fir cones. There are glorious peelings of bark, feathers and fragments of wasp paper, broken china (gathered like uncovered treasure on countless walks) and pockets full of seeds. It is an alchemist's emporium (imaginatively speaking). The magic lies in the imagination that it elicits.

My butterfly collections

Perhaps most pertinent of all to the subject in which this book delights are the butterflies that rest within my collection. They are settled there like ghosts, having been gathered in from quiet places and hibernation spaces where they sought their final rest. Their beauty somehow transcends life; in death it is quite haunting. Their colour has not ghosted. I recall them being poetically referred to as 'children of light' in explanation of their colour resilience. In fact it does, in time, become less vibrant but nevertheless still provides valuable cross-reference when studying hue, if not shade and actual three-dimensional form and scale.

Few textbooks, and I have many magnificent ones, reference the length of a butterfly's leg (or indeed the width of its ankle!) as these specimens do. As my love for my muse deepens, every detail becomes the subject of more and more fascination to me. In terms of pertinence to the creative process itself, that of their artistic depiction, it is invaluable to know, for example, the length of their dainty legs. When forming their likeness in silk-bound wire, it is easy to fail in achieving any near likeness should they be disproportionately long or short (I have personally explored these consequences!). The ultimate in respect of observing detail must be that of looking through a magnifying lens at their miraculous wings, admiring their individual iridescent scales; surely a great impetus to creativity. Again, in respect of allowing close observation to inform creativity, I find myself emulating these tiny scales with miniature stitches across the silken wings of my studies, an exacting yet, for me, immensely rewarding process drawing me a little closer to understanding the miracle of nature.

Artistic technique

Butterflies: beloved by me at first glance and by which, I concede, I am now quite enchanted. As an artist I am compelled by way of that enchantment to employ my creativity to explore the beauty which so transfixes me.

Having studied the intricate patterning of a butterfly's wings through a magnifying lens I perceived that they were made up of tiny scales of iridescent colour, each scale pegged precisely into place; precisely placed yet fine, like dust. As a child I was told that butterflies' wings were covered in fairy dust. As an adult gazing at them through a magnifying lens it seemed I hadn't been far deceived! Yet the truth was more magical still; this 'dust' was in fact pattern, colour and light itself!

Of course, scientifically the structure of butterflies' wings has been long understood. The name 'Lepidoptera', given to the insect order 'butterflies', is derived from the Greek word meaning 'scaly wings'. However I don't think that I will ever step back from the awe of first seeing it for myself, however long it has been understood.

It occurred to me that miniature stitches could, perhaps, depict the detail that I saw, but they would have to be extraordinarily tiny to even begin to describe the beauty of 'fairy dust'. After trial and error, I attempted various feats to enable me simply to see what I hoped to achieve (my optician tells me that as an artist I am working way beyond the design brief of the human eye!). Having discounted jewellers' and dentists' loupes and tripped myself up over various magnifiers sticky-taped to chairs, I settled upon a purpose-built, floor-standing magnifier with an attached daylight lamp. I now find myself settled; my work adequately magnified, my pursuit contented. It is an intensive process, though I rationalise that it takes no longer than the metamorphosis of the butterfly itself (when rationality insists on arguing, commonsense should take precedence over creativity; the two rarely concur). Perhaps it is no more than fitting that my butterflies take so long to emerge.

I begin by painting my wings on to lightweight silk, stabilised with a watercolour primer. This enables me to control the flow of the silk dyes through the fabric. I mix my dyes in a dimpled ceramic palette and leave them to evaporate for a while (long enough to make a cup of tea) into a slightly thicker consistency. Stabilising the fabric is only partially successful in my experience. Fluid dyes are still inclined to bleed, though evaporating some of the liquid from the pigment helps.

The painting process is as unhurried as other processes that I employ, extending to a time frame that many artists would justifiably assign to achieving a finished piece. However, having resolved the painting, the true resolve begins!

Left: Large Blue butterfly (detail from 'Très Fragile', page 74).

Using my handmade needle, I take miniature stitches into the wing fabric, defining and enhancing their painted pattern, adding both vibrancy and subtlety to their colour and shade through carefully selecting fine silk threads from my 'embroiderer's pallet'.

This palette, of fine 20 and 40 denier (some vintage, wound on to handsome wooden bobbins) and lustrous silk floss threads, provides a broad spectrum of colour to choose from. I can separate very fine filaments from the silk floss which I then twist into workable threads, perhaps combining two differing shades into one. When necessary, I also colour my own threads in single lengths with proprietary silk dyes. Frequently changing the colour and tone of thread in the

One of the many tins in which I treasure away my silk threads. This one contains colours echoed in the wings of the Peacock butterfly resting on them. Indeed, this butterfly is the very first one I considered artistically in tiny silken stitches.

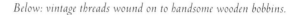

Below: vintage threads wound on to handsome wooden bobbins.

Lustrous silk floss threads providing a broad spectrum of colour to choose from.

needle is unavoidable in the quest to echo the magical patterning, both subtle and startling, of a butterfly's wings. The ends of each worked thread are carefully finished by channelling them back through the stitches on the undersides of the wings. The stitches towards the outside edges of the wings must be closely aligned, angled to follow their form and cover every thread of fabric so as to prevent the wings from fraying when they are finally cut away from the silk.

31

I wire each wing; a hair-fine gauge carefully whipped into place against the stitches on their undersides with an equally fine thread. The wings are then ready to be attached to their respective body.

The bodies are made from an air-drying modelling medium (paper clay or Model Magic®), forming tiny pieces into abdomen, thorax, head and compound eyes. Though I have a number of useful tools for this process I favour using needles (of various gauges), a sharp blade and lengths of wire. It is a process that requires patience. Hurrying at any stage can be woeful; work can be ruined in an instant. Disaster is compounded, somehow, by the work's resemblance to a creature. For me, failure, and I do occasionally concede to it, feels a little cruel!

Modelled butterfly bodies.

Small Tortoiseshell underwings cut from handmade silk paper.

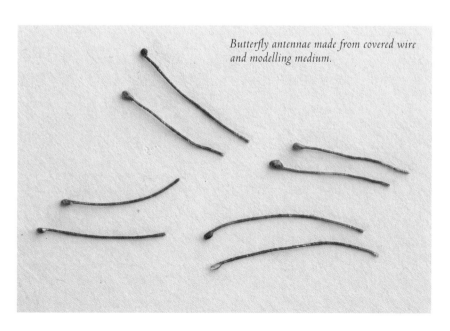

Butterfly antennae made from covered wire and modelling medium.

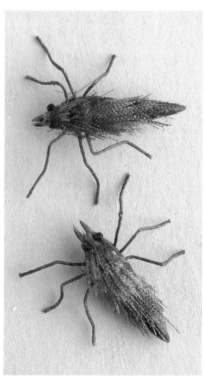

The diminutive bodies are painted with silk dye before being brushed with silk threads.

Here I have added eyes to see, legs to stand them firm and silky butterfly hair to keep them from shivering.

Once dried, I paint the bodies appropriately before brushing whisper-fine threads across them to resemble hair. Each hair tip must first be faintly dipped into solvent-free fabric glue to ensure that it holds fast. Having made little holes during the modelling process, for both antennae and for each of the six legs, I then push these carefully but firmly into place, gently bending the antennae and buckling the legs when they are fixed to resemble their natural form. Both the antennae and the legs are made from covered wire. The familiar clubbed tips of the antennae are achieved by dipping the wire ends into a wet mix of modelling medium, known as 'slip' in modelling terms. I allow them to dry thoroughly before painting.

A little naked body now sits 'shivering' on my desk before I attach its wired silk wings. The tip of each wire must be carefully aligned with its corresponding pre-formed hole. Now, imaginatively speaking, it may take flight and come to rest within a resolved work of art.

Speckled Wood resting on a vintage silk bobbin.

Painting the picture

The scenes against which the flora and butterflies are set are often painted. I work in a similar manner to a watercolourist, except that I use dyes and silk instead of paints and paper. I wash colour as a watercolourist would, with broad, soft brushes and dilute colour. Having then primed the silk (with a watercolour primer), I work in the detail using finer brushes according to the individual considerations of the piece.

'Painted Lady' study, work in progress (see page 116). Thistles, painted with miniature brushes dipped sparingly into silk dyes to illustrate the detail of the plant.

'Periwinkle Wood', work in progress (see page 94). Pins carefully hold drifts of softly dyed chiffon in place against the sketched and painted woodland scene.

In many instances I then begin to enhance texture, diffuse light and create shade within the composition by softly layering the scene with lightweight, often translucent fabrics. I piece them into place to echo or follow the painted form, for example casting shadows within a woodland scene with drifts of softly dyed chiffon or strengthening the qualities of branches and trees with darker, denser layering. The stitches with which I attach such layers are worked all but invisibly by using threads drawn from the selfsame fabrics.

The three-dimensional detail is then finally and securely stitched into place. Using similar methodology I use thread that recedes into the work to become all but invisible. It is imperative that sufficient stitches (a considerable number of them) are taken to afford the piece strength.

'Dreaming', work in progress (see page 110). Slowly, I begin to softly layer translucent chiffon and organza over silk panels painted to suggest the woody qualities of the garden shed.

Habitat

The flowers and leaves amidst which many of my butterflies rest are made from silk. Lightweight habotai and organza emulate the delicacy of many petals, sepals and leaves well. More particularly, silk satin resembles the weight and sheen of such petals as those of the snowdrop. I choose slightly heavier weights of silk to describe stronger or more shrubby leaves.

Lightweight silk habotai is the perfect weight to describe the delicate flowers of the periwinkle. Fine wire stitched through the centre of each petal provides the flowerhead with strength and form.

The silken periwinkle climbs on silk-bound wire stems through the undergrowth of its embroidered world. (From 'Periwinkle Wood', page 94, work in progress.)

I begin with all my fabrics in their natural, pre-dyed state, using proprietary silk dyes to achieve the colour and shade particular to the flower or leaf I am considering. I work as a painter, using dyes to wash across large areas of silk, from which I cut similarly toned petals and leaves, and a miniature brush, dipped in the very same dyes, to control detail. I often paint individual petals and leaves in order to translate their particular qualities, for example the delicate green bows on the spreading sepals of the snowdrop.

The dying and painting process creates the illusion of differing weight through differing shade, from the most delicate to the heaviest. It also gives a little more body to the fibres of the silk, deterring them from fraying. When this deterrent proves insufficient I often use a clear silk gutta (prescriptively used to control the flow of silk dyes), touching it along the cut edges of the petals and leaves with a fine paintbrush. I find this helpful without being too heavy. Otherwise, very cautiously, I use a fray check solution, specifically manufactured for the process. One must bear in mind that this solution is designed especially for preventing seams from fraying; if not cautiously applied with a very fine brush, it can completely bedraggle a tiny silk petal or leaf.

The majority of my petals and leaves are wired through their centres, rather like veining in nature. I carry an appropriate weight of wire through a slim channel that I pinch into the silk against the wire as I work, finely overstitching it into place with a thread drawn from the fabric of the petal or leaf itself. This wire provides strength and affords me the ability to manipulate form into the finished flowerhead or plant.

Stems are invariably silk-bound; a rhythmic, quite hypnotic process, worked by hand, of simply binding from the base and firmly fastening at the tip. At the tip I continue to secure the stamens (often made from fine, knotted silk thread) and the petals of the flower, binding them in with the same thread, then securely fastening at the end. The same process is used to add leaves and buds to the stem.

Each periwinkle stem is entwined naturalistically with another and stitched firmly but invisibly in place.

BUTTERFLY STUDIES

Mine is a field of tousled grasses, a meadow in which to play. A field of dreams where ideas and imagination take flight with the butterflies.

My pursuit of butterflies has taken me along country lanes, through meadows, across downland, deep into woodlands and thickets. I have even crossed the Atlantic, though not with the skill and grace of the Red Admiral, who migrates on gentle wings which belie its strength to spend its summers in Great Britain. It is an inexhaustible pursuit, for I am certain that the sense of joy, excitement and wonder that they engender in me will never diminish.

Throughout the studies that follow I have aspired to share these sensibilities, and I hope that they inspire your pursuit of butterflies, imagination and creativity.

Left: embroidered Brimstone butterfly, resting on a vintage silk bobbin.
Right: the same embroidered butterfly set amidst threads and silk-painted wings pertaining to its study (see page 94).

Peacock Butterfly

Summer Reverie

I recall one summer, at the age of six or seven, picking a little cotton vest out of the laundry basket. As I went to pull it snugly over my head I was startled by a beautiful Peacock butterfly flying out from within its folds. Quite obviously, to me as an adult, it had roosted there before the washing had been gathered in from the line. As a child I was quite certain it was there by magic, confirmed by the fact that the brand label inside the vest was 'ladybird'! To me, then, this was not so far removed from 'butterfly' as to not be magically associated with it. This is, perhaps, my earliest 'butterfly memory'; my mind is so crowded now, with beautiful butterfly memories.

My Peacock Butterfly study illustrates one resting on a plume of buddleia flowers, its wings outstretched, basking in the sun. I could while away hours on a summer's day basking in their beauty, watching their delicate proboscises unfurl and dip into the dainty cups of nectar that the flowers provide.

Size: 36 x 41cm (14¼ x 16¼in)

I was blessed to watch over a hundred Peacock butterflies emerge last summer, my heart leaping as I released them back into the wild.

The Peacock is perhaps amongst the most adept of all butterflies at startling. Its vibrant colours and defensive wing markings are designed to shock, its four false eyes glaring intimidatingly at any threat posed. It must seem formidable indeed to many of its natural adversaries, closely mimicking the notoriously skilled bird of prey, the owl, particularly when, with hind wings uppermost, its body reads like a beak and its outline suggests the bird's familiar ear tufts. It also has the ability to rustle its magnificent wings so loudly as to alert human ears; how deafening and terrifying must that be to a mouse or a hungry songbird! It can even retaliate against harm by emitting ultrasonic 'clicks', achieved by agitating its wing membranes, ensuring that it not be considered a tasty delicacy by bats that may happen upon it whilst roosting or hibernating. Perhaps equal to this battalion of defences is the Peacock's passive ability to all but disappear when resting, such is the camouflage quality of its underwings, akin to the colour and texture of bark. Alas, despite all this armoury, it still often loses its battles.

Of course, this elaborately defensive show is largely perceived by us purely in terms of beauty. The Peacock is undoubtedly considered one of the most beautiful of butterflies. In my eyes, it rivals the glamour of even the world's most exotic species. It is one of our most familiar garden visitors, attracted above all by the flowers of the buddleia. So synonymous is the butterfly with buddleia that I grew up knowing it simply as 'the butterfly bush'. In the wild they favour lucerne, knapweed, thistle, sweet clover and marjoram.

The sole food plant it favours to lay its eggs upon is the common stinging nettle. True to its defensive character, it chooses a plant with the very best defences, a quality that I have felt all too painfully as I have gathered them in to my nursery enclosure for hungry caterpillars. I hasten to add that the very young, very stingy growth is the most delectable of all to them... ouch!

The female of the species will undoubtedly have been engaged by the most zealous of suitors, negotiating her way through many different territories both before and beyond succumbing to the wiles of one. The aerobatics of courtship, flirtation, rivalry and defence, which manifest to human eyes as a beautiful summer ballet in the butterfly's world, surely convey more passion than a Greek tragedy or Shakespearean drama!

She lays up to 500 sticky green eggs on the selfsame young green growth of a nettle. There they rest camouflaged for a week or so. Then, hatching simultaneously, the tiny young caterpillars spin a protective communal web about them, devouring all the leaves within, before repeating the process until they are mature enough to take their chances individually and move beyond it. They continue to live by the adage 'there is strength in numbers' until they are ready to pupate. It would also seem that there is great strength in their formidable spiky appearance; jet black, pin-pointed white – awesome! Alas, this does not deter their most formidable enemy, the parasitic wasp, responsible for the demise of many caterpillars at all stages.

The sole food plant the Peacock butterfly favours to lay its eggs upon is the common stinging nettle. These later hatch into tiny black caterpillars.

The chrysalises that they form are exquisite, varying from mottled parchment grey-brown in woody environs to golden green, speckled magenta when suspended amongst leaves.

The study

The study was begun by painting the buddleia on to a piece of silk organza, first washed in a summery green shade. The flowerheads, stems and leaves are subtly depicted in the distance, the detail becoming more focused around the butterfly itself.

Using petals as patterns, I cut tiny organza flower shapes, shading them buddleia mauve by barely dipping my miniature paintbrush into appropriately mixed dyes and allowing them to flow out to the petal edges. When dry, I stitched them into place on the flowerhead using fine silk thread in a vibrant shade of pollen yellow. Lifting some of the petal edges to rest against each other I grouped some areas tightly together, achieving gentle three-dimensional relief.

A larger-than-life watercolour sketch of the Peacock butterfly enabled me to clearly define its colouring and wing pattern, realising a better understanding for its rendition in stitch.

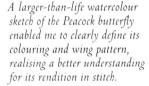

On my studio desk I collect my thoughts and deliberate over my resources. A pen-and-ink sketch, whose simple lines enable me to clearly define the buddleia plant's structure and form; a resolved embroidered butterfly; a scattering of painted wings and a selection of appropriate threads — an artist's musings manifest.

43

I then defined the stems of the plant, outlining them in stem stitch (how very appropriate!). Having strengthened the composition by way of surface embroidery I then drew it forward visually by stitching three-dimensional silk leaves in place at appropriate junctions along the stem, simply catching the fine-wired leaf stalks down with threads of an identical shade.

Having strengthened the composition by way of surface embroidery I then drew it forward visually by stitching three-dimensional silk leaves in place at appropriate junctions along the stem.

Finally, the summery picture is ready to receive its silken-winged summer visitor, the Peacock butterfly. A miniature silk painting, detailed with miniature silk stitches to emulate wing scales, carried on a tiny body borne of paper clay, its dainty legs and delicate antennae, silk-bound wire. A member of a brand new lepidopterous family, artistically discovered, akin to nature, and evolved in honour of nature.

Red Admiral

Field Study

Herald of the summer; ennobled by its handsome garb; uniformly patterned red, white and black, as admirable as any livery. It is no wonder that the eighteenth-century name bequested to this butterfly was 'Admirable' or 'Alderman'. Admirable indeed is its migratory journey each spring from Southern Europe to Great Britain. Arguably the strongest-flying of all British butterflies, it makes its epic journey across land and sea without ceasing over the course of two to three weeks. Scientists, awed by its mastery of flight, have discovered that it spins and swirls the air across its wings to create turbulence, dexterously using passive and active upstrokes and rotating its wings. Equally marvellous is its inherent ability to use the sun as a compass and discern the most advantageous flight path; taking sheltered lees over land and high thermals and following winds above the sea.

My Red Admiral Field Study depicts the butterfly as I admired it one summer's day amongst the tousled grasses of the field.

Size: 22 x 47cm (8¾ x 18½in)

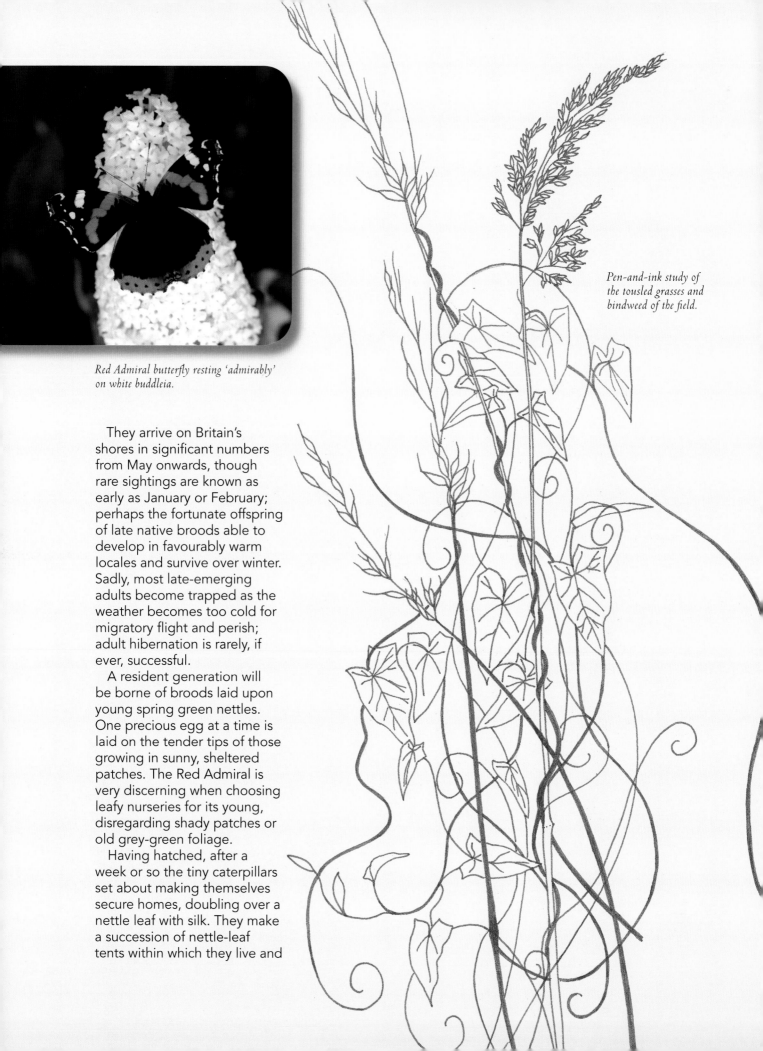

Red Admiral butterfly resting 'admirably' on white buddleia.

Pen-and-ink study of the tousled grasses and bindweed of the field.

They arrive on Britain's shores in significant numbers from May onwards, though rare sightings are known as early as January or February; perhaps the fortunate offspring of late native broods able to develop in favourably warm locales and survive over winter. Sadly, most late-emerging adults become trapped as the weather becomes too cold for migratory flight and perish; adult hibernation is rarely, if ever, successful.

A resident generation will be borne of broods laid upon young spring green nettles. One precious egg at a time is laid on the tender tips of those growing in sunny, sheltered patches. The Red Admiral is very discerning when choosing leafy nurseries for its young, disregarding shady patches or old grey-green foliage.

Having hatched, after a week or so the tiny caterpillars set about making themselves secure homes, doubling over a nettle leaf with silk. They make a succession of nettle-leaf tents within which they live and feed, hoping to avoid harm. When they are ready to pupate they construct 'the marquee of all nettle tents', incorporating two or three leaves, some times even felling the whole tip of the nettle, buckling it over with silk. Alas such 'nettle marquees' are conspicuous to their raffish adversaries – parasitic flies and wasps. One species, the black ichneumon wasp, is, I am assured, particularly elegant and interesting and entirely dependent on its butterfly host. I remain equivocal. I would rather delight in the admirable adult butterfly, hypnotically fanning its wings whilst enjoying fallen fruit or the sweet nectar of its favourite flowers, amongst which are buddleia, seedum, michaelmas daisies, clover and scabious – such exquisite taste!

The study

My Red Admiral Field Study depicts the butterfly as I admired it one summer's day amongst the tousled grasses of the field. Initially, I washed the silk the colour of summer straw, mottling it whilst damp

A swatch of silk threads chosen to describe the colour and pattern of the Red Admiral in stitch.

An embroidered Red Admiral rests on the corner of my butterfly journal describing its admirable beauty. Threads used in its study rest alongside.

with a deeper shade, playing with the quality of light which seemed to dance with the butterfly that day. It was settled at the margins of the field where the bindweed swirls about the grasses; this was my next subject, detailing its twisting, clasping growth with paintbrush and dye pallet. I then highlighted certain stems with silk stem stitch. Tassels of silk floss, formed by knotting different shades, snipping the knots off at their bases and teasing out the tails, were then stitched against the painted grasses to illustrate seed heads. Three-dimensional stems of grass, silk-bound with translucent organza leaves and knotted silk seed heads, were then introduced together with bindweed, comprising wired organza leaves, silk-bound tendrils and stems. I favoured the use of translucent silk in the three-dimensional detail to maintain the illusion of light.

Finally, the intricately hand-embroidered butterfly was introduced, poised to rest against the bindweed and grasses, with the illusion of air beneath her wings, suggesting that she has yet to settle. Perhaps it is silk stinging nettles she seeks.

Opposite: the embroidered butterfly is secured to the silk-bound wire stems of the bindweed, holding her away from the surface of the work and thereby creating the illusion of air beneath her wings.

Flowering stems of wild grass described with tassels of silk floss. These were formed by knotting different shades of silk together, snipping off the knots at their bases and stitching them on to silk-bound wire stems before resting them against the painted field study and securely stitching them in place.

Red Admiral

Wishes

The golden petals of the dandelion flower radiate like the sun; closing at night like tightly folded parasols on dull days. In seed, they rise like the moon, delicate globes, resplendent with light. Just a breath of air disperses them to become a galaxy of shooting stars. From childhood I have wished upon these stars, scattering them with all my puff. I was encouraged to tell the time by them, too. Many will know these beautiful seed heads as 'dandelion clocks', counting the number of puffs to blow all the seed away. I rarely counted beyond two o'clock – two puffs, a perfect hour of the day, allowing for plenty more play time!

The Red Admiral is to me synonymous with lazy, late summer days, blowing dandelion clocks to tell the time rather than referring to my watch. This piece is reflective of such a wistful summer's day.

Size: 27 x 41cm (10¾ x 16¼in)

The study

The dandelion was painted on to lightweight silk, initially stabilised with watercolour primer to prevent the dyes from running. I then traced the outline and mid-vein of the prominent leaf and the dandelion stem in stem stitch, using sheeny silk floss to catch any light falling on the study. I used vintage silver thread and fine threads drawn from a length of habotai silk to detail the painted seed heads, taking long stitches against the brushstrokes. French knots worked in silver, olive and white silk built body into the seed head, against which I attached three-dimensional seeds.

A swatch of silk threads and photograph clippings describe the qualities of the Red Admiral that I endeavour to convey artistically.

A corner of my studio, in which an embroidered Red Admiral rests on the corner of my journal, a glass jar of 'wishes' (dandelion seeds), to be cast on rainy days or special occasions, beside it together with reels of silk used to stitch the butterfly's wings.

The three-dimensional leaves are cut from silk habotai, sheer organza and chiffon dyed appropriate shades of dandelion green. The dandelion leaf is a splendid pattern to trace. The dandelion is in fact so-named due to the resemblance of its sharply serrated lobes to the teeth of a lion; from the French, *dent de lion*. Equally, one could liken the flower petals to a lion's mane; a playful thought, arguably no less valid lexically.

Wishes, blown like kisses, falling, coming to rest, growing into dreams.

Dandelion leaves, their splendid 'lion's tooth' pattern traced on to silk habotai and organza, their sharply serrated lobes cut with sharp scissors.

The feathery parachutes of the dandelion seeds, described with threads drawn from various weights of woven silk fabric bound together on to fine wire. French knots worked into the painted seed head define its structure and sharpen the focus of the study.

The feathery parachutes of the individual seeds are described with threads drawn from silk satin, habotai and organza, drawn together and bound on to lengths of fine wire. The wire is in turn bound with silk floss. Each seed is stitched into place against the painted and embroidered seed head with the same shade of silk floss, the stitches thus disappearing into the picture.

The study is set both within and forward of a dark green mount. The mount is covered with silk fibres, teased across and beyond its surface so as to 'cloud' the central image. The technique of creating such papery cloth from silk fibres is best described as paper making. The fibres must be over-laid and adhered to one another to create an interesting surface or useful material. It is best to use a cellulose-based glue for this purpose.

Far left: dandelion seeds scattered across the mount as if blown from the dandelion clock central to the study.

Left: dandelion leaves cut from shimmery silk paper 'ghost' across the dark green mount.

I generally work on a large sheet of plastic, lifting the papery silk cloth from its surface when it is dry before incorporating it into the study. In this instance I brushed it with opalescent dye to enhance shimmer. Leaves cut in silhouette from this shimmery fabric further over-lay the mount to interrupt its solidity and unify the composition.

Finally, our 'autumn admirable', the Red Admiral, takes its place. Tiny stitches secure it beside the timeless dandelion clock.

This image, taken across the work, illustrates the natural lift of the butterfly's wings and the soft, feathery quality of the dandelion seed head.

The Red Admiral's intricate patterning, described in miniature silk stitches, is clearly visible in the magnified image.

Holly Blue

Silent as Light

'Strolling country lanes this afternoon I found my absent-minded gaze at once distracted when, in the twinkling of an eye, I glimpsed fragments of heavenly blue sky scattered about the hedgerow. Stealing closer, I perceived not fallen sky but sky-blue wings; the sylphy Holly Blue butterfly, playing in the fleeting sunlight'.

Butterfly diary excerpt: September 2010

Sky blue, glimpsed in the twinkling of an eye, skipping about hedgerow canopies in the sunshine, the Holly Blue is perhaps the most familiar blue species of British butterfly. A familiarity undoubtedly promoted by its predilection for holly; as its namesake suggests. Though equally appropriately it could have been named the 'Ivy Blue'.

My Holly Blue study illustrates two dainty female butterflies resting on ivy, perhaps considering laying eggs to become second-brood caterpillars of the 'silken species', peculiar to rarefied artistic climes!

Size: 23 x 45cm (9 x 17¾in)

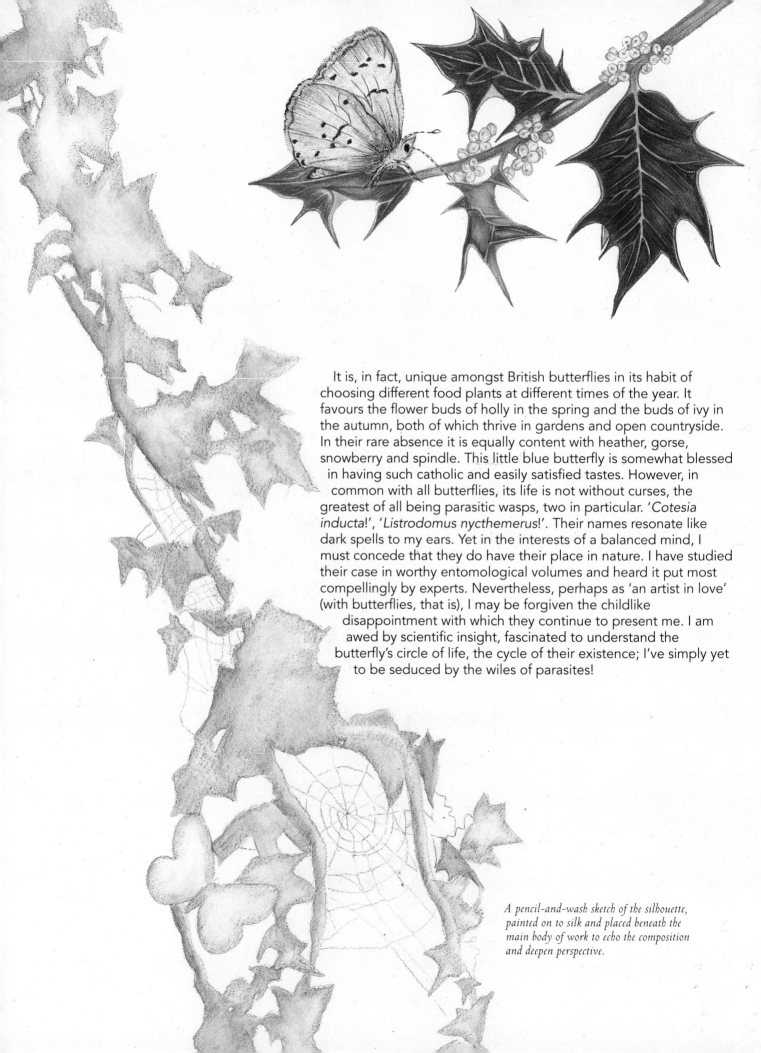

It is, in fact, unique amongst British butterflies in its habit of choosing different food plants at different times of the year. It favours the flower buds of holly in the spring and the buds of ivy in the autumn, both of which thrive in gardens and open countryside. In their rare absence it is equally content with heather, gorse, snowberry and spindle. This little blue butterfly is somewhat blessed in having such catholic and easily satisfied tastes. However, in common with all butterflies, its life is not without curses, the greatest of all being parasitic wasps, two in particular. '*Cotesia inducta*!', '*Listrodomus nycthemerus*!'. Their names resonate like dark spells to my ears. Yet in the interests of a balanced mind, I must concede that they do have their place in nature. I have studied their case in worthy entomological volumes and heard it put most compellingly by experts. Nevertheless, perhaps as 'an artist in love' (with butterflies, that is), I may be forgiven the childlike disappointment with which they continue to present me. I am awed by scientific insight, fascinated to understand the butterfly's circle of life, the cycle of their existence; I've simply yet to be seduced by the wiles of parasites!

A pencil-and-wash sketch of the silhouette, painted on to silk and placed beneath the main body of work to echo the composition and deepen perspective.

Those that do not succumb to the advances of parasites gorge on fresh berries, camouflaged in berry-coloured caterpillar suits. Once fully grown they become true masters of seduction, creatively speaking; I find their extraordinary ways most beguiling. Their advances are, however, designed to attract not artistic whimsy, but the attention of particular ants with a penchant for the honeydew they produce and a natural yen to protect its source. As chrysalises, they continue to hold the protective attention of the ants with provision of these sweet secretions and, much to my awe and wonder, a sweet song played out by the gentle agitation of their abdominal sections, mimicking the sound of 'antkind'. The ants, quite understandably, often carry their sweet and tuneful charges into the heart of their brood chambers where they tend them until they emerge as adult butterflies, at which point they process them like carnival queens back out into the open countryside where the magical cycle begins again. A tale of such wonder; to me illustrating perfectly the adage: 'truth is stranger than fiction', inspiring my butterfly muse all the more.

The study

My Holly Blue study illustrates two dainty female butterflies resting on ivy, perhaps considering laying eggs to become second-brood caterpillars of the 'silken species', peculiar to rarefied artistic climes!

The embroidered Holly Blue butterfly settled amongst some of the threads, watercolour pencils and brushes used to describe the beauty of its natural counterpart.

They were fashioned by painting, then minutely stitching their silken wings, attaching them to tiny, modelled, paper-clay bodies with silk-bound legs and antennae. They rest against ivy leaves cut from lightweight silk dyed verdant green. The leaves are wired through their mid-veins, all but invisible stitches catching a very fine wire tightly in place through a channel pinched into the silk as I oversew. These wired leaves are bound and stitched into a delicate bough comprising wire bound with ribbons of dyed silk fabric. Ivy tendrils are suggested with silk-bound wire contorted to rest naturalistically amongst the foliage.

Here, much magnified, the miniature stitched scales of the Holly Blue are clearly visible. So too the stitched mid-veins of the ivy, carrying a fine wire beneath the leaves which enables me to manipulate them naturalistically within the composition.

Right: at even greater magnification, the stitches are more apparent still. A dainty knotted silk web can also be glimpsed beneath the butterfly's hind wing.

Delicate spiders' webs are 'spun' at forks in the bough. They are worked by travelling very fine threads from one point of the bough to another, creating a wheel of spidery spokes which I then proceeded to weave another thread through, knotting it against each silken spoke as I worked, creating firm yet fragile spidery webs.

Below: a strong bough realised in twisted wire bound with torn silk ribbons holds the delicate spiders' web fast. Each radiating thread of the web is secured at the back of the bough. Another thread, woven and knotted against the spidery silk spokes, resolves the web.

A shadow, just visible in this image, is cast beneath the web and bough by echoing the silhouette of the study under the main body of the work.

The camera glances across the butterfly's wings, revealing the dimension of the study.

Large Blue

A Spell Amongst the Wild Thyme

Through a soft mist, still drifting from the shoulders of dawn, draping across the wooded valleys and sleeping villages along our journey, we made our way in hushed excitement to seek the rare Large Blue butterfly. Like treasure hunters, we had marked our map with a cross, placed as accurately as possible on the spot where we hoped to find it: a south-facing hillside in Somerset. A place where wild thyme, the particular food plant of the butterfly, grows and where the grass is grazed as it was in ancient days, to the liking of a certain red ant. Upon this ant the extraordinary Large Blue 'casts a spell', beguiling it to nurture it through its caterpillar stage to pupation and beyond, to its ultimate emergence on the wing. It is perhaps this magical symbiosis coupled with the butterfly's rarity and beauty that, in turn, casts a certain spell on butterfly enthusiasts.

This study depicts the butterfly alighted upon wild thyme; reflective of the very summer's afternoon on Collard Down that I was visited by the elusive blue beauty.

Size: 26 x 26cm (10¼ x 10¼in)

The air was still when we arrived on Collard Down. It was too early for the flutter of wings. We had been eager to arrive before the butterflies began to stir, to delight in their environment from first light. The hillside was cast with spiders' webs, spun like dreamcatchers as if to entangle the sleeping hillside's bad dreams, allowing only good to prevail. Indeed, it was dreamy here in the most idyllic sense. The whole hillside sparkled as if covered with shisha mirrors as the dew-drenched webs caught the climbing sunlight. The wild thyme, strewn like soft scatter cushions across the landscape, blushed the colour of dawn sky. I felt so content; contrived though it may sound, I began to wonder if I was awake or perhaps still dreaming.

As the day properly dawned so too did our realisation that we were arguably too late in the butterfly's season to seek a treasured sighting; they are on the wing for only four to five days of the year. Our worthy butterfly guidebook identified the fact and a notice board that we came across set on the border of the nature reserve confirmed it.

We brewed coffee on our travellers' stove and rested, adjusting our expectations to simply enjoying the beautiful environment about us;

Large Blue resting on sedge.

Large Blue sunning its slightly tattered wings.

any sense of disappointment swiftly evaporated with the morning dew. We wandered the hillside, now in brilliant sunshine, admiring so many species of butterfly – Marbled Whites, Skippers, Meadow Browns, Commas, Peacocks and Red Admirals – before settling to rest for a while in the dip of the hill. I sat on a tuffet of grass beside some wild thyme and watched a bumble bee clumsily nuzzling the dainty flowers for nectar. Then, out of the corner of my eye (where magic hides) I glimpsed a flutter of blue; a flutter of blue which then danced in to settle on the very thyme I was admiring. It was, in fact, a Large Blue butterfly! I was now convinced that I must be dreaming, so disbelieving was I that this could be true. But the camera never lies and with the swiftness of its shutter I had captured a true sighting! This elusive beauty had, it seemed, sought and found me – a reconfirmed day-dream believer!

The Large Blue butterfly, though the largest and rarest of the native British blue species, has a diminutive wing span of just one and a half inches (about 4cm). Discovered around 1795 it was prized by butterfly collectors for its rarity and beauty, and consequently hunted to near extinction by the 1920s. Thereafter its demise was furthered by agricultural change, with much of the Large Blue's very particular habitat being destroyed by ploughing and seeding. Suitable breeding sites unstricken by the plough were rendered hopeless by the introduction of yet another agricultural policy, namely that of infecting the country's rabbit population with myxomatosis. It transpired that unless the breeding sites of the Large Blue were appropriately grazed to a height that suited the survival of a certain red ant, *Myrimica sabuleti*, this beautiful butterfly was doomed to fail entirely, for it is upon this remarkable relationship that it depends for its survival.

The relationship between the Large Blue and *Myrimica sabuleti* is indeed remarkable. Having laid her eggs on the young flower buds of wild thyme, the minute larvae hatch and burrow into the flowerheads, feeding on the flowers and developing seeds. Having grown to just a milligram or so in weight, they then fall to the ground and wait to be discovered by foraging ants. They lure the ants to them by producing a honey-like secretion from special glands. Having become quite intoxicated (I suggest in less than scientific terms) by this liquor, the ants are duped into believing that the tiny caterpillar is in fact a queen of their kin and hurry off with her to their nest where they continue to care for her like royalty. Once inside the ants' nest the caterpillar becomes predatory, feeding on the ant grubs therein, continuing its deception of the colony by emitting a scent which mimics that of the ants' own. Under these conditions the caterpillar rapidly grows to a size at which it is comfortable to hibernate, to resume its activity the following spring. There is growing evidence to suggest that it may continue its existence within the ants' nest for up to two years. In time, having consumed upwards of a thousand ant grubs, it is ready to pupate.

The formed chrysalis exists within the nest for a further three weeks, emerging as a butterfly with, science tells us, a burst of song! Though, as an artist, some may consider me fanciful (one could even say that I professionally 'embroider' the truth) this is surely 'fact stranger than fiction'. The Large Blue actually serenades the ants that host it throughout its life stages, with sound or 'song' closely mimicking that of a queen ant. As it emerges it sounds, as it were, a royal fanfare and, with all the attending pomp and ceremony, the ants commence to process the newly emerged butterfly out of their nest into the morning sunshine where it makes its way, with ants in attendance, up into the tussocky grasses. There it clings, fully inflating and drying its wings, before taking flight. Thus this remarkable story begins again.

Thanks to the pioneering work of conservationists, prominently Professor Jeremy Thomas, this story is again enacted in Britain. Having realised an extraordinarily comprehensive understanding of this delightful butterfly's needs, he has pioneered the successful reintroduction of several new colonies to carefully managed sites in the South of England, such as Collard Down in Somerset where I sought and found my inspiring sighting. This inspiration is manifest in two Large Blue butterfly studies.

A swatch of silk threads, painting and photograph clippings, exploring the qualities of the Large Blue and its habitat.

Right: swatch, silk threads and photographs from our spell of time on Collard Down exploring the beauty of the Large Blue. An embroidered butterfly rests on my favourite water dipping pot, which I employ in my silk painting.

The study

This first study depicts the butterfly alighted upon wild thyme; reflective of the very summer's afternoon on Collard Down that I was visited by the elusive blue beauty.

The wild thyme is painted using silk dyes on to lightweight silk. I used a miniature paintbrush befitting the subject; arguably the tiniest flower that I have ever studied, barely a fairy's breath of pink to each four-petalled flowerhead. Likewise, I rendered the dainty green leaves and wispy grasses. With ambition to preserve the delicacy and softness of the wild thyme, I determined not to stitch into the painting, however restless my needle, instead focusing the detail into my observation of the butterfly itself, placing it in three-dimensional relief against the painted flower study. Familiarly, the butterfly has delicately painted and embroidered wings, carefully underwired with hair-fine copper wire and attached to a miniature body modelled from an air-drying medium, painted then brushed with silk fibres. As I work with such fine components, I often focus upon the grace and poise of the butterfly itself; it stills my mind and engenders the delicacy of touch necessary to succeed. Perhaps one could argue that it is a form of meditation; certainly, rather than vexed, I invariably feel very calm whilst I am working.

With miniature paintbrush I sought to convey the delicacy and softness of the wild thyme, barely dipping into the petal-pink dye to illustrate each flowerhead. I also used the tinest of brushes to describe the fairy's breath grasses in the distance. The three-dimensional grasses comprise fine, silk-bound wire 'tufted' with blush-pink and green silk fibres.

Right: the butterfly, in three-dimensional relief, against the painted flower study.

Large Blue

Très Fragile

This Large Blue study finds its inspiration in happy summer days spent with friends in France. Neil and I were invited to share some time with them there at their home, in ancient days the site of an old quarry. The original quarry buildings have now been sympathetically restored and converted; the surrounding land, lovingly and intelligently managed to provide a haven for butterflies and other wildlife. Here sightings of the Large Blue, though none-the-less thrilling, are less elusive than in the South of England.

The antique paper in which this gold leaf was wrapped, its contents denoted with the delicately scripted words 'très fragile', had always appealed to my romantic sensibilities as much as my sense of artistic purpose. It was satisfying to employ both these qualities in the presentation of this piece.

Size: 45 x 45cm (17¾ x 17¾in)

It was during this summer, with the guidance of my friends, that I gained the confidence to identify the Large Blue from other blue species. It had long seemed to me that all blue butterflies were alike on the wing; exquisite fragments of summer sky. Little by little, however, with the help of my butterfly friends, I began to appreciate the difference. The Large Blue, uniquely, has inky black spots on the upper side of its fore-wings and clearly defined white wing margins. It also has a familiarly laconic flight, variously described in guide books as 'floppy, slow and fluttering'. Having spent time with the Large Blue in the South of France, I would say, in empathetic tone, 'relaxed'.

The study

The antique French gold leaf, against which this embroidered Large Blue is set, had been treasured away for years in a corner of my studio, waiting to present such a story: the 'très fragile' blue butterfly, borne in my memory of blue-sky summer days in France and treasure-hunting expeditions to Somerset.

Right: the embroidered Large Blue butterfly poised upon the treasured book of French gold leaf.

Left: resting upon the corner of a precious leaf of gold, my artistic rendition of the exquisite Large Blue butterfly. Threads used to embroider its dainty wings rest beside it.

Speckled Wood

Spirit of the Woodlands

Here, I feel beauty, tangibly. I do not simply perceive it about me, I am suffused with it. Suffused with the divine brightness of the bluebells, I am at once in ecstasy and at peace.

Here, I breathe the very breath of spring; redolent, reviving.

A soft rain of birdsong falls through the greening woodland canopy and drenches my mind. Abstracted, untroubled, it now holds nothing but melody.

The sun shines lovingly, lingeringly about me.

My eyes are bright, brilliant with wonder as the azure sea of bluebells laps into their very corners. I focus to trace the downward arch and supple grace of a single flower stem scrolling from the earth; beside it another and another. Such immanence, such an eloquent message writ. I read; exceeding intrinsic peace, and feel wise.

Speckled sunlight gathers into wings which alight the flowers. Thirsting for nectar, the butterfly drinks then dances away. By and by I shall follow but for now the wisdom of this woodland holds me still.

Lines from a Bluebell Wood

My homage to the Speckled Wood aspires to portray one of my most beloved butterfly havens; a coppice within strolling distance of my studio in Dorset, which in springtime is awash with bluebells, a heavenly blue sea filling every hollow of the woodland floor, lapping against the trees.

Size: 50 x 20cm (19¾ x 7¾in) approximately

The speckled wings of this delightful little butterfly are perfectly companioned to the speckled light which percolates through the woodland canopy. Males keep vigil over particularly radiant patches of sunlight, poised to woo females drawn to it, territorially chasing away any other male suitor who may deem to 'steal their spotlight'. The tussle ensuing from such trespass is, it seems to me, aptly compared to a stage performance; their spiralling dance, ascending into the woodland canopy, is a joy to watch. Females tend to hide away demurely in the tree tops, descending only to nectar on flowers in spring and autumn and, otherwise, to meet their suitors. A plentiful supply of sweet honeydew coating the leaves in the tree tops satiates their appetite during the summer months. They often draw their suitors away from the spotlight, up into their tree-top haven, to satisfy their appetite for love too.

A Speckled Wood butterfly resting on a leaf displaying its exquisite underwings.

The female lays her precious eggs singly on the leaves of various grasses, including cocksfoot and couch grass. They hatch within seven to ten days. Spring and summer broods are fully grown and ready to pupate within a month, forming beautiful green chrysalises beneath grass blades or in nearby vegetation. They remain in perfect suspension for another month before emerging as butterflies on the wing. The Speckled Wood is, however, unique amongst butterflies for its ability to overwinter as caterpillar or chrysalis. Caterpillars emerging in the autumn will live through the winter, feeding during mild spells, and pupate the following spring when fully grown. Chrysalises formed in the autumn will delay pupation until the following spring, emerging in unison with the first nectar-rich flowers of March. It is thus that the Speckled Wood can be seen for eight to nine months of the year, successive generations gently overlapping. An individual butterfly lives just twenty days.

The eighteenth-century name for the Speckled Wood was 'Wood Argus', so-named after the many-eyed hero of Greek mythology, Argus himself, affording the butterfly a sense of myth and mystery. 'Speckled Wood' resonates with me as the very best name for this spirit of the woodlands. When I delight upon one, be it in the garden, along the lane or on the common, it instantly transports me to an idyllic woodland glade speckled with sunshine.

My homage to the Speckled Wood aspires to portray one of my most beloved butterfly havens; a coppice within strolling distance of my studio in Dorset, which in springtime is awash with bluebells, a heavenly blue sea filling every hollow of the woodland floor, lapping against the trees.

The study

I have considered the bluebells and the Speckled Wood butterflies set amidst them entirely three dimensionally, housing the study within an antique glass dome. A sense of dimension – of 'breathing space' – is always important to me artistically. I aspire artistically to share a 'breath of fresh air', simplistically speaking; this is surely what we all step out into nature to enjoy.

An embroidered Speckled Wood resting against reels of silk used to describe its dainty wings in delicate stitches. The handmade needle used for the purpose, still threaded, rests beside it.

Modelled bluebells stand in a tall, slim bottle, found whilst walking in the countryside. Alongside are silk threads used in my bluebell study, modelled flowerheads and wistful, wizened bluebells from a previous spring.

The bluebells are modelled from an air-drying modelling medium known as Model Magic®, though there are similar mediums on the market including paper clay, which I also enjoy working with. This particular medium dries to a similar weight and quality as the silk which I use in conjunction with it. Each flowerhead is modelled from a petal-fine fragment of the medium, scoring and dividing each of the five petals whilst keeping them intact, abutting each other. I then draw them together into their characteristic bell shape over the tip of a miniature paintbrush handle before persuading them to curl subtly and naturalistically upwards with the aid of a bodkin, before leaving them to dry. Their stamens are worked in knotted silk, each flower being allocated five, according to my observation of the flower itself.

Having knotted the stamens I then thread them through the modelled flowerheads and attach the ends to fine-wire stems. These stems are then bound to the main flower stem with silk floss thread. I join in the delicate silk spathes that are characteristic of the plant as I work. This process is repeated along the whole length of the bluebell stem until I reach its tip.

The number of flowerheads on a bluebell stem varies considerably; I have counted up to fourteen on the longest stems that I have represented.

Bluebells, their modelled petals cupping knotted silk stamens. The flowerheads nod gently on delicate stems of silk-bound wire, conjoined with silk sepals at the strong, tapered silk-bound wire stem.

When all the flowerheads are bound in place I then gently coax them to hang appropriately, finally arching the bluebell stem to stand gracefully and naturalistically within the composition.

An assemblage of a dozen or so modelled bluebells, together with their long, strap-like leaves (worked from silk with wire overstitched through their mid-veins) undoubtedly befits the visit of two silken Speckled Woods! The butterflies have painted and intricately embroidered silk wings; diminutive modelled bodies painted and brushed with silk fibres; fine, bound wire legs; and clubbed antennae – in common with all my 'silken species'. They are suspended with the aid of leaf-green, silk-bound wires discreetly attached to their undercarriages and hidden amidst the leaves.

Finally, beneath the bluebells rest fallen leaves: beech, oak and hazel, as if scattered by the preceding autumn. They are cut from silk habotai and dyed autumnal shades. The veins of many are detailed with stem stitch and many are wired invisibly, enabling me to curl and twist them with regard to nature. In turn, these leaves rest against the woodland floor; fragments of silk and heat-distorted synthetic chiffons, suggestive of the rich earth.

The whole study in practical fact stands 'rooted' in a shallow dome of creatively disguised Styrofoam™, affirming that all artistry must have a practical, methodological root.

Silken species of Speckled Wood butterflies suspended amidst the bluebells with the aid of leaf-green, silk-bound wires hidden amongst the foliage.

Beneath the bluebells rest embroidered silk leaves as if scattered by the preceding autumn.

In common with all my silken species, the Speckled Wood has painted, intricately embroidered wings; a dainty modelled body brushed with silk fibres; fine, bound-wire legs and clubbed antennae.

Orange Tip

Sunrise

A cold, late February day of squally showers and sunshine. The sun, when it deems to shine, glances everything with catkin-yellow light, beatifically dedicating all it touches to spring; leaf buds tipping branches, hedgerows, meadows, open spaces, hidden places ... human spirits. Beneath the birches snowdrops flourish. Cupping the sun, imbued with light, they hang like lanterns held steadfast on straps of verdant green. They light a train of thought away from dark places, travelling beyond winter's station to lively days. Days when, heralded by birdsong, the sun rises and sets softly. Spring days, budding anew, exuberant with flowers, alighted by butterflies.

Butterfly diary excerpt: 'butterflies on my mind'.

My Orange Tip study illustrates the butterfly softly gliding across a cloud of silk fibres as if to alight upon a cluster of snowdrops.

Size: 27 x 41cm (10¾ x 16¼in) approximately

'Orange Tip' is perhaps too literal a name for one of the prettiest of British butterflies. More fittingly it is known as *'Aurora Falter'* or 'Sunrise Butterfly' in Germany and *'L'Aurore'* or 'Rising Sun' in France; names I prefer to call to mind when I chance upon this shining beauty.

One of the earliest butterflies to emerge each spring, overwintering as chrysalises, they can be seen as early as March. Though I have never seen an Orange Tip alight on snowdrops, I keep the promise that 'it is possible' close to my heart, particularly on cheerless, wintry days. Possible, that is, in my whimsical, creatively biased mind, snowdrops can certainly be seen flowering into March and I know with confidence that their nectar is particularly sweet and alluring.

The males, with their sunrise-orange wing markings, are first to emerge, patrolling the countryside in search of the females of their species. The females are far more elusive; with demure, pencil-grey tips to their wings they rest camouflaged in hedgerows and thickets before conceding to be courted, only taking to the wing, having mated, in search of food plants on which to lay their eggs. Whilst resting with their underwings closed, males and females share the same exquisite, moss-like camouflage, keeping them a little safer from prying, predatory eyes. Of course, nature isn't given over entirely to vanity in terms of the handsome orange markings of the male; they are designed not solely to impress coquettish females but also to warn predators of the distasteful mustard oils ingested by the butterflies at their larval stage from their food plants, such as garlic mustard. It is unlikely that any hungry predator would suffer more than a peck or nibble of this bitter-winged (albeit beautiful) snack per lifetime.

Orange Tip resting on a primrose, painted on to silk, signed and defined in stitch.

Newly emerged Orange Tip resting on the laurel hedge, opening and closing its wings to catch the fleeting April sunshine.

There are a good many different species of white butterflies by which the amorous male Orange Tip may be confusedly lured, indeed I read that they have been observed to investigate 'anything white'! However, they do have a discerning sense of smell and the female Orange Tip has a very distinctive scent; any dalliance along the way is swiftly and unceremoniously dismissed.

The female is very particular about where she lays her eggs, choosing flowering crucifers along hedge banks, field margins, rides and glades. She initially recognises the plants on which to alight by sight, confirming her choice by way of extraordinary sensory cells on her feet, able to detect the chemistry of the plant. She unfailingly chooses flowerheads with plentiful seed pods, conscious of the voracious appetites of her young, and is careful not to lay on a plant that already bears an egg; as the caterpillars are cannibalistic by nature, the consequences would by woeful.

The eggs are spindle shaped and, in poetic unison with the adult 'Sunrise Butterfly', slowly change in colour from opalescent white through pink to deep orange over the course of two to three days. They are ready to hatch after a week or so, whence they burrow into a flowerhead and feed on the developing seed before becoming exposed along the seed pod. Initially, the caterpillar wears a conspicuous, long-haired, black suit which it soon sloughs off in favour of beautiful, bluish-green garb in perfect camouflage with the plant on which it rests and feeds.

Leaving their food plants to pupate, they hang in exquisite form, hidden amongst tall vegetation or within bushes, and adopting either vibrant green camouflage colouring or, less commonly, pale brown. The adult butterfly graces our days for little more than a fortnight; rarely is there more than one generation a year.

89

The study

My Orange Tip study illustrates the butterfly softly gliding across a cloud of silk fibres as if to alight upon a cluster of snowdrops.

The silken sky across which the butterfly glides is effectively silk paper stretched across a mirrored surface. I worked the paper by layering silk fibres across a sheet of heavy-duty plastic before brushing them softly with dilute PVA glue. Once dry, I removed the resulting wispy material ready to employ it as a background to my study.

A swatch of silk threads bound alongside a photographic section of an Orange Tip's wing, exploring its colour and patterning in readiness to stitch.

An Orange Tip butterfly set amidst the silk threads used to describe it in stitch. Three snowdrops with silk-satin sepals and green-tipped, silk-habotai petals rest in a glass vase.

The snowdrops have silk-satin sepals and green-tipped silk-habotai petals with very fine wires stitched through their centres. The petals are drawn together to enclose a cluster of hand-knotted silk stamens and bound on to wire stems with Japanese silk floss, concentrating the binding at the bulbous head of the flower before smoothly binding down to the base. Emulating nature, a small, leaf-like spathe is bound into place to cover the tip of the flowering stem.

The strap-like green leaves are cut from appropriately dyed silk habotai and wired through their mid-veins to stand proudly amongst the flowers.

The green-tipped, silk-habotai petals of the snowdrop glimpsed from beneath the flowerhead. The detail has been painted with the finest of strokes using a miniature brush barely dipped in green dye.

The three-dimensional quality of the snowdrops amidst their verdant green leaves. Careful wiring of the petals, stems and leaves enables them to stand proudly away from the surface of the piece.

The flowers and leaves are secured to the wispy background using all but invisible stitches, taken individually, each securely knotted to anchor the detail firmly in place. There is considerable disparity between the weight of the flowers and leaves and the wispy cloth against which they are stitched, making this process imperative to the integrity of the finished work.

The stems and leaves are nestled into a tangle of ivy and mossy green threads. The ivy is cut from appropriately dyed silk organza and habotai. Each leaf is wired through its mid-vein, the wire then bound to resemble the leaf stem and caught with a single knotted stitch against the background fabric. Fine threads teased from mossy green silk crepe are stitched to tumble around the leaves, creating the illusion of softness and depth.

Finally the 'Sunrise Butterfly' is carefully stitched into place, ensnared by its tiny, silk-bound legs using delicate stitches caught into its ethereal silken sky. This tiny butterfly was such a joy to consider and honour in stitch. I found that the perfect shade of silk could only be derived from a single filament of 'sunset orange' Japanese silk floss.

Above: the flowers hang like lanterns held steadfast on straps of verdant green.

Left: a tangle of ivy and mossy green threads, in which nestle the snowdrop stems and leaves.

Right: the Orange Tip glides softly across a cloud of silk fibres.

Brimstone Butterfly

Periwinkle Wood

A country mile or so from my studio there is an ancient copse where periwinkle flowers are strewn like earthbound stars shining brightly against a verdant green sky. They are visited there by a beauty more radiant still, The Brimstone butterfly. Resplendent as the moon, bright as the sun, she rides her woodland galaxy with beatific grace. This ancient woodland keeps the Brimstone secret through its long winter sleep in the evergreen cover of its ivy-clad trees. Brimstone butterflies seek such refuge as autumn yields to winter. In tribute to their tenacity, they can still be seen on the wing into the cool days of early November. They are also amongst the first butterflies to emerge each spring, being coaxed from hibernation by warm sunny days, sometimes as soon as late February or early March. The longest on the wing each year and the longest lived of all British species, it can survive up to a year, fate permitting.

The Brimstone is the namesake of all butterflies, called 'bottor-fleogre' in Anglo-Saxon times, meaning butterfly or 'buttery fly', due to its buttery coloured wings. Fables were told of them stealing butter and cream from the dairy, further defining its name.

Size: 49 x 88cm (19¼ x 34¾in)

Primroses and purple flowers are favoured in the springtime, amongst the earliest of which is the periwinkle. The Brimstone's long, delicate proboscis is particularly adept at drinking from its long flower tubes. It is observed that the butterfly's head, antennae and legs may have evolved to become the same colour as the blooms to protect them from spiders that live within. They settle contentedly for considerable spells of time, supping from the delicate flower chalices, wings folded, silent as the sun.

In the hedge banks bordering the woodland, the female seeks buckthorn and alder buckthorn on which to lay her precious eggs. She lays but one at a time, being particular to choose sheltered, sunny spots close to leaf buds or on the tender growing tips of unfurling leaflets, befitting the appetites of her young. There they will feed, grow and hopefully keep from harm's way until they realise their time to pupate.

The study

I began this study by painting the Brimstone butterfly's glorious yellow wings in preparation for settling to stitch their miniature scales in pauses taken from working on the woodland scene within which it would take its place. The butterflies are undoubtedly the most exacting and time-consuming element of my studies. I find that it best suits me to work on 'the bigger picture' in conjunction with such detail, balancing my creative energy. The Brimstone's wings

A periwinkle flower with silk-habotai petals, a bright, white-painted iris and fine, yellow silk pollen at its centre, described with frayed silk threads.

Below: the beautiful Brimstone butterfly, its glorious yellow wings described with miniature stitches taken in sunshine yellow, sunrise orange and woodland green silk.

rested on my embroidery frame, slowly gaining silken scales each day; not, alas, by magic or the miracle of metamorphosis, but by human hand alone; my own. Sylvan scene and sylph were realised in unison, give or take a stitch in time.

The silk against which the woodland is depicted was first washed faintly with yellow dye, reminiscent of sunlight and of the Brimstone itself. I then sketched in the trees, enhancing their form and suggesting their texture using pencil and graphite-grey shades of dye applied in a painterly manner.

A swatch exploring the beauty of the Brimstone wings.

An embroidered Brimstone rests amidst the makings of its delicately stitched wings. Further wings, held on my embroidery hoop, slowly gain silken scales.

Having established the structure of my woodland I then began the gentle process of layering lightweight, translucent chiffons and organzas across it, hand-stitching them in place. By controlling the density and shade of the layering I was able to evoke light, deepen shadows and build texture.

I emphasised the root structure at the base of the trees with deeper, darker layers. Their trunks and branches were established similarly, using lighter layering in moderated tones. Lightest of all, the air itself is suggested with whisper-fine, threadbare organzas and chiffons caught down in drifts across the scene.

I have described fallen wood in the foreground of the piece, against which I have set the trailing periwinkle. I achieved this by making very fine silk paper from combed silk tops, pulling it about to distort it as it dried to hold texture and form akin to bark and branch. Once dry and ridged, I stitched it into the woodland scene in my familiar practice of using tiny stitches in appropriate shades of fine silk. I then established the area further by over-laying it with sheer chiffon, invisibly stitching it in place using thread drawn from the chiffon itself.

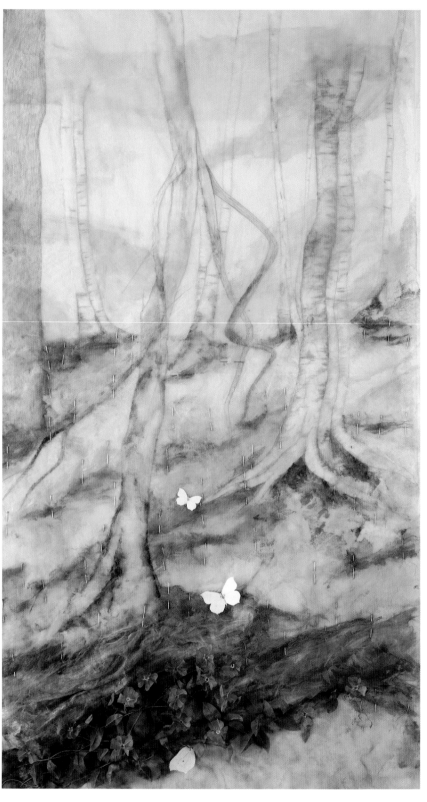

Periwinkle Wood, in the process of being layered with lightweight, translucent chiffons and organzas to evoke light and shade and build texture.

The periwinkle petals are cut by hand from lightweight silk habotai and then painted appropriately with silk dyes, paying particular attention to the white iris around the centre of each flower. The flowers are borne singly on silk-bound wire stems with wired silk leaves bound in at intervals along each length. Each periwinkle stem is entwined with another naturalistically and stitched invisibly but firmly into place.

Fallen wood in the foreground of the piece, described using fine silk paper moulded and distorted as it dried to hold texture and form akin to bark and branch.

The trailing periwinkle set against the fallen wood.

Three Brimstone butterflies take to the wing within the silken woodland scene. The first rests upon the periwinkle. When resting, Brimstones always hold their wings together, their underwings beautifully camouflaged as yellowing leaves. They have beautifully defined wing veins which I have detailed with a slightly heavier denier of yellowed green silk worked in dainty back stitch. The scales are detailed in finer denier silk, subtly changing from yellow to green, rethreading the needle accordingly as I worked. Their characteristic orange wing spots and the traces of darker colour at intervals along their wing margins were a joy to observe in appropriate shades of thread.

Below left: Brimstones always hold their wings together when resting, as do all butterflies. The Brimstone's underwings, with their beautifully defined wing veins, provide perfect camouflage in the guise of yellowing or sun-lit leaves.

Two Brimstones, receding in scale, are stitched into place as if fluttering into the woodland scene. I am always delighted by the early spring light that glances Britain's woodlands; Brimstones often appear to me to be fragments of sunshine itself.

Having 'metamorphosed' through the processes of painting, embroidery and modelling, the Brimstone butterfly is rested and secured in place; the signature of the piece.

Small Tortoiseshell

Sleeping Beauty

A 'butterfly letter' to welcome you home:
It's been another glorious day here in Dorset, beaming with every ray of golden light that the proudly brilliant autumn sun could boast. Neil and I enjoyed a ramble across to East Knoyle at the weekend ... kicking through fallen leaves ... watching them dance like fairies from the trees. Fluttering from a hedgerow, one became – or just possibly was already – a butterfly. One of the 'aristocrats' I think, possibly a Small Tortoiseshell, no doubt searching for a quiet, dry corner in which to roost and hibernate.

Excerpt from a letter to a dear friend.

My Small Tortoiseshell hibernation study illustrates the butterflies sleeping in a woody environment: the corner of my garden shed.

Size: 29 x 29cm (11½ x 11½in)

I was blessed to host several quiet gatherings of Small Tortoiseshell butterflies through their winter hibernations when I lived in my aerie at Chettle House. As autumn drew on, a dozen or so would gather to form a tawny brown cloud in the soft, sky-blue corner of my kitchen. They would rest there, just touching wings as if to reassure each other; their dainty legs, like unblinking eyelashes, steadying them. I was careful not to disturb their long winter sleep, and month after month they would remain there, perfectly still, butterfly dreaming. They only stirred from their stasis if the air was warmed coaxingly by over-enthusiastic oven roasting or baking. This was rarely an issue; my quarters were cosy but not in a centrally heated sense. Any warmth created soon dissipated, rushing away on keen draughts and into the nooks and crannies which make a manor house built in around 1710 'characterful'! More aptly, and to my great delight, it was normally the alluring warmth of the following spring that woke them, when I would hear them tapping politely against the windows to be released.

The Small Tortoiseshell is perhaps the most beloved of all British butterflies, gracing gardens across the nation with its beauty. As autumn falls it aspires to come in from the garden and take up winter residence in hibernation within homes. More than any other British species, the Small Tortoiseshell is inclined to live in close companion with man. Alas, 'man' or, more pertinently, well-meaning housekeeper, is often inclined to unsettle the butterfly intent on its long sleep; perhaps behind the curtain in the spare room or in the

Small Tortoiseshell nectaring on creeping thistle.

cool corner of the ceiling, to release it back into the garden from where it must once again seek refuge somewhere cool and dry, in the process using up valuable energy reserves. Garages and sheds often prove to be more successful choices.

The butterflies wake from hibernation during the first warm days of spring; from mid-March onwards. Their energies restored by the sweet nectar of spring flowers, their new resolve is to realise the next generation. They become active from around ten in the morning. The males are intent on finding a territory to settle by 'the top of the morning' (around noon). Most will be patrolling such a site: a sheltered spot, preferably south facing and close to a lush patch of new nettles; 'the ladies' favourite'. In hot pursuit of any butterfly trespassing on it or any female seductively winging by, the male will hold this territory for up to ninety minutes. If during this time he has not been lured by the chase of a suitable female, he will set up another territory which he will patrol for a similar length of time, again depending on what romantic opportunities may arise!

A successful encounter with a passing female may lead to a chase lasting two or three hours (perhaps she is testing his commitment and endurance!). Small Tortoiseshells are indeed very strong flyers; typically they fly approximately one and a half miles (about two and a half kilometres) a day. Furthermore, it is a migratory species, with migrations recorded across the Atlantic in both directions, though more typically it is migrants that swell the numbers here in Britain rather than British-born butterflies migrating abroad.

Having successfully mated, the female will then go, or more aptly 'fly', to great lengths in pursuit of a perfect site in which to lay her eggs. She is very particular, seeking out only the youngest, most tender nettle plants, growing in full sun on the edges of large nettle beds. She lays sixty to eighty eggs at a time on the underside of a nettle leaf. This same leaf may well be visited by another female, and another; up to a thousand eggs have been counted grouped together, piled atop each other. Tiny green and black caterpillars hatch ten to fourteen days later. Forming groups of approximately two hundred, they feed gregariously, spinning a protective web about themselves that encloses the growing tips of several leaves. Once these are devoured, the process is repeated. It is understood that in grouping together in this manner they are also able to regulate their body temperature. The caterpillars become solitary as they mature towards pupation, developing protective spines to deter predators. Alas, this defence is not altogether adequate; they make tasty and nourishing snacks for songbirds and nothing, it seems, deters their nemesis, the parasitic fly. The Small Tortoiseshell is vulnerable to parasitic attack throughout its early life stages. Some flies inject their eggs directly into the soft, fleshy caterpillars; others, in particular *Sturma bella*, lay their eggs divisively close to the young, avidly feeding caterpillars, which unknowingly proceed to ingest them.

Spring buttercups provide a welcome source of nectar after the Small Tortoiseshell's winter sleep.

Those that reach pupation are found perfectly suspended beneath the eves of buildings, against walls or under the more protective cover of hedgerows. They are exquisite both in colour and form, ranging from lilac pink to brown; copper washed and bronzed. Alas, still appetising to birds and vulnerable from within from previous parasitic attack, not all will realise life on the wing. Every new butterfly is, it seems to me, both a miracle of nature and of survival.

The study

My Small Tortoiseshell hibernation study illustrates the butterflies sleeping in a woody environment: the corner of my garden shed. I considered rendering their setting in sky blue, akin to their favourite corner of my kitchen. But however settled they were there, in that quiet corner, once upon a time, as I translated the scene artistically

Swatch of silk threads used to define the colour and patterning of the Tortoiseshell butterfly's wings.

An embroidered Small Tortoiseshell resting on a reel of silk, used to describe the scales adorning the butterfly's wings. Other silks used in this endeavour are also shown, together with a wispy silk web and an embroidery hoop holding a silk butterfly painting.

my silken butterflies seemed most unsettled in such a context. The memory of the real sleeping beauties, 'soft clouds in the kitchen sky', perhaps more befittingly still drifts freely in my butterfly dreams.

The woody environment favoured by hibernating butterflies comprises strips of lightweight silk treated in such a way as to be reminiscent of shed panelling. This I achieved with the use of dye crayons, rubbing them over the silk whilst resting it against the shed panels themselves. Many a time have I paused to consider how eccentric my artistic pursuits may seem, particularly when shut in the garden shed, rubbing at the walls! I then refined these rubbings with further washes of silk dye before tearing the silk into strips and folding it in the fashion of wood panelling, with one sharp-sawn (in this instance folded) and one rough-sawn (torn) edge.

Having stitched these panels to gently overlap against a lightweight silk backcloth, I then set about creating a sense of light and shade, of unswept corners and secret dusty spaces. I achieved this by over-laying the silk panels with fragmented, sheer synthetic chiffons dyed to both subtly merge and contrast with the panelling. Stitching them in place with threads drawn from the chiffon itself ensured that the stitches all but disappeared into the work.

Settling the sleeping beauties in place. Here the Small Tortoiseshell's painted silk wings are temporarily pinned into place in consideration of where they will finally rest within the composition.

Together with this diffusion, this sense of illusion, I also incorporated spiders' webs, though not of spider silk but of knotted silk threads and wispy silk fibres. I wove my webs by first knotting fine denier twisted-silk thread across an embroidery hoop. Having constructed the foundation of my webs in this fashion I then drifted fine wisps of silk tops across their surfaces using very dilute glue to set them in place. A great deal of experimentation was necessary to achieve my spidery webs. Throughout my endeavour, I bore in mind the saying: 'if at first you don't succeed, try, try, try again' (attributed to Robert the Bruce who, having sought refuge from battle in a cave, watched a spider spin its web and felt duly inspired by its perseverance). A worthy sentiment for all those in pursuit of artistic satisfaction, whatever their medium.

Having realised an environment befitting hibernating butterflies (those of this particular 'silken subspecies', that is) I then set about settling the sleeping beauties in place: two groups of three, one preferring solitary sleep and one startlingly awake.

Spiders' webs of wispy silk drift across the composition. A solitary wing is caught like confetti in the gossamer threads of one. Undisturbed, three butterflies are still sleeping, whilst one is startlingly awake.

The sleeping butterflies' folded wings are carefully painted with miniature paintbrushes and silk dyes appropriate to their camouflage colouration. A hair-fine wire is stitched along each wing margin, concealed at the back of the work, affording the wings sufficient strength to stand and hold their form. Each butterfly has four wings, stitched and paired through tiny modelled bodies that are painted and brushed with silk fibres. They each have six tiny legs with which to steady themselves within their environment and dainty clubbed antennae.

The wide-awake butterfly, in startling contrast to its subdued background, has painted and embroidered wings worked with careful consideration of the wing pattern and colouration of the Tortoiseshell butterfly itself, employing techniques familiar to all my butterfly renditions.

A scattering of single wings rests across the piece, representing the 'butterfly confetti' scattered by the mice in whose company the butterflies dare to sleep.

Sleeping butterflies, with carefully painted wings stitched and paired through tiny painted bodies. Each butterfly has six tiny legs to hold it steadfast whilst it sleeps with the aid of the tiniest of stitches to anchor them securely.

The wide-awake butterfly, in startling contrast to its subdued background and sleeping fellows.

Peacock Butterfly

Dreaming

Five species of British butterfly are known to hibernate as adults, including the Peacock and the Small Tortoiseshell. Having stored as much nectar as possible during the days preceding their hibernation, they seek out dark, sheltered spaces, affording them as much protection as possible from the elements and the attention of predators. They favour sheds and attic spaces, cool, indoor rooms or adequately roomy holes in trees. They are known to congregate in large numbers; naturalists have counted upwards of forty gathered together, perhaps affording them greater protection from predators (according to the adage 'there's strength in numbers'). This is surely the intent of the Peacock butterfly, which is capable of issuing a disconcerting hissing sound that, amplified in numbers, is surely more terrifying still. However, by the same token they can often be found – when they can be found, that is – in solitary sleep.

Perhaps ready to take flight from its long winter sleep, or possibly startled awake prematurely, one butterfly rests with resplendent open wings, their pattern and colour conveyed by way of silk painting and the minute depiction of individual scales in stitch.

Size: 37 x 37cm (14½ x 14½in)

Alas, many fall prey to the appetites of their predators, in particular 'mousekind' and tidy-minded mankind, and some are lost to damp and disease, but to popular delight 'a sufficiency' (in my heart there could always be more) re-emerge each spring and continue their glorious circle of life.

Once upon a time I lived in a beautiful Queen Anne manor house in the quiet village of Chettle in Dorset. A spiral staircase hewn of stone, worn smooth over history by generations of footsteps intent on serving the needs of the manor and its nobles, lead to my quarters – and beyond, into the dark and secret exposed attic space.

Occasionally, particularly when I returned home late at night, I would fearfully contemplate what may lurk there. Imagination can be both friend and foe! However, a certain benevolence pervaded my sense of space there and any unsettling whim or fancy always retreated swiftly. I was more inclined to consider what blessed creatures may live up there: mice keeping happy families (conceding that their brutish ratty cousins may visit sometimes, which would account for the occasional 'bump in the night'); bats, whose dance I delighted in watching from my windows on moonlit nights; swallows tucked under the eves; beetles, with their distinctive tappity tap; nightmarish to building conservators and best thought of all, 'hibernating butterflies'.

Peacock and Small Tortoiseshell butterflies nectaring on buddleia.

I knew for certain that there were butterflies up there, sleeping through the long, winter months. I knew this because each year a sprinkling of butterfly-wing confetti was bestowed upon the stairs; evidence, alas, of those who had not survived their winter sleep, undoubtedly falling prey to the appetites of the creatures with whom they shared their winter retreat. Those wings that I discovered I treasured away; unfadingly beautiful, I have them to this day. Yet more beautiful and vibrant still, the memory of the butterflies that I helped to rediscover the light each year, nursing them in cupped hands down the spiralling stone steps and out into the garden, releasing them, 'nobles of the attic', into the sunshine.

The study

I have considered hibernating Peacock butterflies in a very similar fashion to the hibernating Small Tortoiseshells. The panelling against which the Peacocks are settled is somewhat heavier, standing more proudly from the surface of the work by means of laying medium-weight wadding beneath them. The panelling then recedes softly, an illusion achieved by means of dropping the weight of silk to a single layer.

An embroidered Peacock butterfly resting on a needlework box amidst a selection of silk threads used to work tiny silk stitches across its wings.

The layering of fragmented chiffon and silken spidery webs across this panelling is all but the same as with the Small Tortoiseshell study, though two of the webs are more predominantly woven and knotted before being diffused with silk fibres.

The resting butterflies were constructed to stand entirely three dimensionally before I placed them on their sides within the composition, as if clinging to the rough-hewn edges of the panelling. I anchored them there with minute stitches, being careful not to pull them down too firmly in order to preserve a naturalistic stance.

Perhaps ready to take flight from its long winter sleep, or possibly startled awake prematurely, one butterfly rests with resplendent open wings, their pattern and colour conveyed by way of silk painting and the minute depiction of individual scales in stitch. In similar fashion to all my butterflies, it has a dainty modelled body, painted and brushed with silk fibres, six tiny, bound-wire legs and dainty clubbed antennae.

Several single wings caught up in the composition illustrate the demise of butterflies that do not wake from their long winter sleep.

Considering where to rest the sleeping butterflies, I carefully pin their folded wings in situ within the composition.

The resting butterflies, constructed to stand entirely three dimensionally, now rest naturalistically within the composition.

A butterfly rests with resplendent open wings, their colour and pattern conveyed by way of silk painting and the minute depiction of scales in stitch.

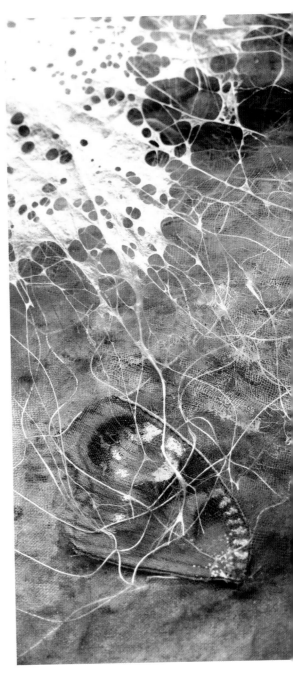

A single wing caught up in a spidery web, illustrating the demise of butterflies that do not wake from their long winter sleep.

Painted Lady

Thistledown Summer

As summer days lengthen towards harvest time, the air begins to swirl with seed: thistledown, willowherb and dandelion drift on the softest breeze. Rebuking 'tidy-minded gardeners' anxiety' (a terrible affliction!), I delight in looking out from my studio across the field to watch them stealing up into the sky, their downy parachutes sparkling in the sunshine as they tumble towards their decent.

Finally, after careful consideration as to which flower, leaf or stem seemed fitting for her to grace, the butterfly itself found its place within the composition.

Size: 23 x 37cm (9 x 14½in)

One summer, a strident patch of thistles flourished their seed prolifically about the field, which gathered in drifts on the ground like fairy snow. It was argued that it would prove a great menace the following year when the thistle patch would be seen to advance across the whole field. True enough, the fairy snow melted to give rise to a sea of mauve thistles, but then who should advance across this ocean to bob about in it but the Painted Lady butterfly – indeed, not one but hundreds! Menace? No, the absolute antithesis.

The very year that our field became a sea of thistles an unprecedented migration of Painted Ladies reached Great Britain. During the last weekend in May 2009 an estimated twenty-eight million crossed the southern coastline, fanning out across the country, reaching as far north as the Shetland Isles and even beyond into Iceland. Their journey brought them from far away; namely the desert edges of North Africa and south-west Europe. Hundreds of miles away from our field in Dorset. Further still, the journey of those that continued north, with sightings reported the phenomenal distance of about 1800 miles (3000 kilometres) north of their winter breeding grounds! Such a distance perhaps commanded the commitment of several generations along the way; scientists who study such phenomena are still agog!

Ink-and-watercolour sketch of creeping thistles, to be transposed on to silk.

When breeding conditions are optimum, Painted Ladies emerge in great numbers, rising up in vast migratory clouds from their winter breeding sites to seek cooler climes where they will give rise to further generations. Small numbers can arrive as early as January or February along the south coast of Great Britain, though more commonly they arrive from late May to June. Their preferred food plant is the thistle, occasionally choosing mallow or nettle, though their caterpillars struggle to thrive on such alternatives. They lay their eggs singly on the upper sides of the leaves where they rest for a week or so before hatching into tiny caterpillars that then crawl beneath these 'nursery leaves' and proceed to gather a tent of leaves about them. Securing their shelter with silk, they feed upon it until all but the toughest leaf-ribs remain. They then begin the process again until, finally, they are ready to pupate.

The plump caterpillars rest openly for a while on the plant on which they feasted before forming into magnificent chrysalises. Burnished, gold- and bronze-like jewels, they secrete themselves within larger tents of vegetation; perchance to avoid the admiring, avaricious glances of predators.

This whole process plays out over a four- to six-week period, allowing for more than one new generation to emerge during a favourably hot summer. These summer beauties are either destined to make the return journey back across the Atlantic to their winter breeding sites, or sadly perish as summer yields to autumn and temperatures drop to below five degrees centigrade, which they are unable to survive.

Painted Lady nectaring on buttercups.

The study

My Painted Lady study illustrates the butterfly resting against a painted and embroidered backdrop of thistles. The painting was achieved in my usual manner: employing miniature paintbrushes dipped sparingly into silk dyes to illustrate the detail of the plant, against a colour-washed piece of lightweight silk habotai primarily stabilised to prevent the dyes from flowing freely through the silk fibres.

I then proceeded to embroider into the painting. First, I 'sharpened' the edges of the leaves by tracing them with a fine silk thread, worked in simple back stitch. In the same fashion I detailed the flower stems and the strong mid-veins of the leaves.

Silk, stretched and colourwashed, was then stabilised before I painted the thistles with miniature brushes dipped sparingly into silk dyes. I was careful to observe the detail of the plant — so delicate and yet so spiky!

I then embroidered the thistle flowerheads; working single knotted stitches in Japanese silk floss, bringing the cut ends of the stitches forward and teasing out the separate filaments of each thread with my needle to suggest the lightness and texture of the flowers in the field.

The delicate grasses were worked with fine wire, silk threads and a considerable amount of patience! Binding such fine wire with even finer thread whilst binding in filaments of Japanese silk floss at each of the cut ends to represent the flowering seed heads was as challenging as it was rewarding.

Filaments of floss silk teased out with my needle satisfyingly resemble the lightness and texture of the flowers in the field.

Dainty grasses patiently achieved by binding super-fine wire with even finer silk. Binding in filaments of Japanese silk floss to represent flower seed heads was as time consuming as it was rewarding.

Rather than feeling vexed during such tasks, I realise my reward by focusing determinedly on the particular miracle of nature that I am observing. The generally simply understood and often overlooked beauty of a single stem of grass surely illustrates the miracle of nature as eloquently as the most exotic of flowers when closely admired. Once accomplished, I stitched the grasses into place within the context of the piece using all-but-invisible, single knotted stitches.

Finally, after careful consideration as to which flower, leaf or stem seemed fitting for her to grace, the butterfly itself found its place within the composition. I often indulge a playful sense of disassociation from the accomplishment of the work at this stage, and consider the butterfly to be independent of the creative process, a creature in and of itself. By that token, I allowed the silken butterfly itself to decide where it should rest, imaginatively

The embroidered Painted Lady butterfly rests against the silk threads employed to represent her miniature wing scales.

bestowing it with a freedom akin to that of the very butterfly which inspired its creation. In truth, artistically one knows when the balance of a piece is right. It is not at all fanciful to say, however, that this is an art in itself. I have often been known to determine that a butterfly doesn't look 'happy' where I have chosen to rest it within a piece and move it; the ultimate decision has, in fact, been known to take days. One needs to be patient with oneself as well as with the processes one employs 'in the making'.

The making of the butterfly itself commanded hours of minute stitching in faithful observation of the scales of real butterflies' wings. These wings were then wired invisibly beneath the stitches and drawn together on to a diminutive body moulded from an air-drying medium, painted and brushed with silk fibres. The antennae and all six legs are silk-bound wire.

A glimpse beneath the Painted Lady's wings affords an insight into the three-dimensional quality of the piece.

Aurelian Butterfly Collection

Aurelian, the archaic word for a lepidopterist or butterfly enthusiast, seemed a fitting title for this study; a collection of butterflies. Throughout history, the aurelian has enthusiastically collected precious specimens of butterfly from the wild; a practice which challenges my sensibilities, and those of many delighted by them in nature and invested in the cause of conserving them on the wing rather than in collectors' cases, statically pinned.

Many early naturalists published their collections in books which have now become collectors' items themselves, valued for their scientific insight and exquisite illustrations. This study is a homage to the spirit, if not the practice, of these extraordinary individuals.

Size: 26 x 49cm (10¼ x 19¼in)

Orange tip ~ Anthocaris cardamines

Holly blue ~ Celastrina argiolus

Red admiral ~ Vanessa atalanta

Orange tip ~ Anthocaris cardamines

Peacock ~ Inachis io

Holly blue ~ Celastrina argiolus

Brimstone ~ Gonepteryx rhamni

Lesser periwinkle ~ Vinca minor

Peacock ~ Inachis io

Chrysalis
Inachis io

Orange tip ~ Anthocaris cardamines

Live butterfly collecting, with the exception of when it is deemed necessary to the furtherance of science and conservation, is a pursuit justly frowned upon today and to my great relief little indulged. The modern-day collector is more often intent upon simply gleaning 'sightings'. The camera has largely replaced such paraphenalia as pins, ether and killing bottles, once considered essential to the butterfly hunter, making 'capture' as swift and benign as the motion of the lens shutter. Furthermore, many modern lenses have far greater reach than old-fashioned butterfly nets, telescopically drawing elusive beauties closer, and magnifying or macro lenses afford the modern-day aurelian phenomenal insight into the exquisite detail of their quarry.

Orange Tip, Anthocharis cardamines.

Peacock butterfly pupae, modelled from air-drying modelling medium.

Brimstone, Gonepteryx rhamni.

However, modern-day aurelians arguably owe a debt of gratitude to their founders; the intrepid explorers, collectors and illustrators of Lepidoptera responsible for establishing the foundations of our knowledge. Many early naturalists published their collections in books which have now become collectors' items themselves, valued for their scientific insight and exquisite illustrations. This study is a homage to the spirit, if not the practice, of these extraordinary individuals.

Right, from top to bottom: Holly Blue (Celastrina argiolus)*, Red Admiral (*Vanessa atalanta)*, Peacock (*Inachis io)*.

Index